4 Steps to Social Media Marketing for Crafters

A toolbox to make selling crafts online easier

Sakina Murdock

KerCHING! Marketing Books

Published by
KerCHING! Marketing Books
Cumbria, UK.

Special thanks to: Saddaf Hussain, Leigh Cunningham, Yvonne Higgins, Lindsay Capps, Kevin Beynon, Monique Snyman, Anne Nichols, Freepik.com.

Cover art by Monique Snyman.

Contents

29 Step 2: Set up your social media accounts and your shop

What's your craft?

Whatever you make, if it's original and handmade, you can sell it.

Follow these straightforward steps to take aim at your market, catch customers' attention, and rake in a bit of cash. Ramp up your efforts and go full time if that's what you want!

The potential for this information to change your life is huge, and though there are no quick answers and truly secret formulas, you'll find plenty of 'get started' help and advice in here.

We've gone for a plain English, jargon-free style to make it easier to read, and you won't find masses of detail or complicated explanations here. It's fundamentals only! Your success will be down to all the effort and time you put into the job. It's all your work, no-one else to blame or take the credit.

Social media marketing is like crafting. You don't need to know everything to get going. Start with the basics and the rest will build with experience.

This book is for crafters who want to test out going full time with their skills, and for those who spend more on materials than on their kids! It's even for savvy people who had a go at selling already, but didn't have the time to make it work, or found it too expensive.

The information here is useful for any crafter who wants to sell their wares, whether it's paper cutting, doll making, shoe painting, knitting, or bottle making. Everything in here is a tool to set you off on a practical marketing journey, step by step through social media.

Where you go with it is up to you.

Hand-cut confetti by Leigh Cunningham

MeriMakesUK

facebook.com/MeriMakesUK

STEP 1

Choose the right social media sites for your crafting business

When you're not a natural salesperson, it's easy to get lost, fed up, or bogged down when you try selling the things you make.

You just want to make stuff, right?

But selling your gorgeous crafts is an exciting step towards making 'stuff' full time, so it's a hurdle totally worth overcoming.

Where better to start, than on the social media sites you already use?

The secret is to use the social media sites that will work best for you and your new business.

That way you'll be in reasonably familiar territory, but sometimes you'll have to learn something new.

Right now, you need to think about what you do, and understand what you want to get from selling your lovely crafts online.

Let's go!

Prep Task 1: what you do, and why

Grab a pen and a notepad, or just use the notes space on these pages, and answer these two questions:

1. What do you produce?

Write a single line to describe your crafting products. Use some describing words too, like 'lovely', or 'cute', or 'beautiful'.

Example: I make cute outdoor fairy gardens, or I make saucy stamped metal key fobs, and stunning silver jewellery.

2. What do you want to get out of selling your crafts?

Think about why it will be worth the time and effort. What's the real reason? Job satisfaction, achievement, or a living wage?

Example: I will be able to make a proper income from making and selling my soft toys, or I will be able to justify spending all my cash on crafting.

Who will buy your wares?

To get started, you only need a rough idea of your audience.

For example:

- *Their gender.*
- *Their age range.*
- *How well-off they are.*

What are demographics?

Demographics describe groups of people who are similar in some simple way.

For example:

- *Women.*
- *Men between 30-45 years old.*
- *Expectant mothers.*

Most research about social media users focuses on a few basic characteristics, so when you think about your audience's demographics, keep it simple for yourself.

Take expectant mothers: they're a clear demographic, but you'll struggle to find data that shows new mums use a particular social media site (other than Mumsnet). However, you *can* aim at women between 18-45.

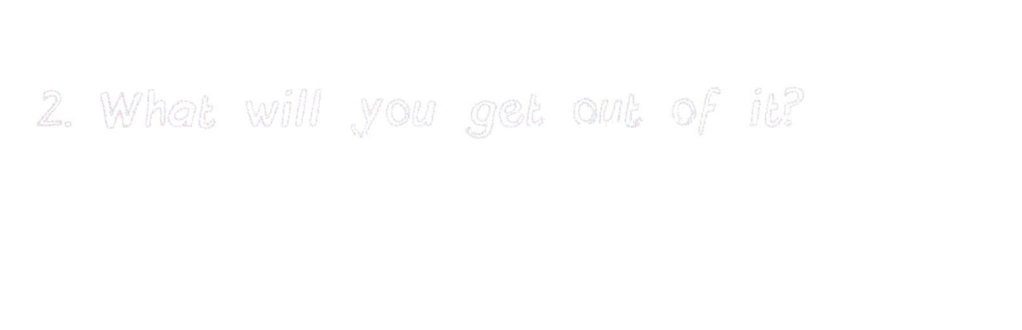

Prep Task 2: Figure out your audience

Think for 30 seconds: Who will buy your work? Who would you like to target?

You don't need to survey your Facebook friends - just make it up!

Choose any target audience you think will like your goodies and will have the money to buy them. Those people are your market. Later, when you create online ads, you'll aim directly at them.

It's important your chosen market can afford your products, so join up the dots carefully.

For example: young mothers in their 20s might love those little crocheted blankets with matching bobble hats for their babies, but will they be able to afford £20-30 for that?

Could you be better off aiming at first-time mums aged 30-39? Just a thought.

This can be hard, so take your time. There's room for mistakes and you can tweak things later. Nothing's ever really ruined by cloudy thinking early on - you'll always get the chance to amend your ideas at another time when you've learned a bit more.

If it helps (doesn't work for everyone) imagine the whole person: their families, jobs, and their need for your products ... whatever stokes your imagination.

Flip your notepad open again, or use the notes space on the following pages, and answer these questions about your audience:

1. What gender are they?

2. How old are they?

3. What are their jobs?

Use this process to figure out which social media sites will be best for you, and how to use them more effectively.

That way you don't waste time and money you could have spent on crafting.

2. How old are they?

3. What are their jobs?

Not feeling confident?

It doesn't matter at this point if you get it wrong, or feel uncertain; later you'll be able to test things out one bit at a time, until you're sure you understand who will look at your promotional ads.

Notes

Where is your audience?

Your audience hangs out somewhere online.

According to Pew Research Center's *Social Media Usage 2005-2015* and *Social Networking 2013* statistics:

Almost everyone is on one social media site or more.

That's why we love social media as a place to make more friends and connections, and to sell more stuff.

And it's not just about the younger crowd, although that's the obvious part about this graph. Every other age group has a serious presence online too.

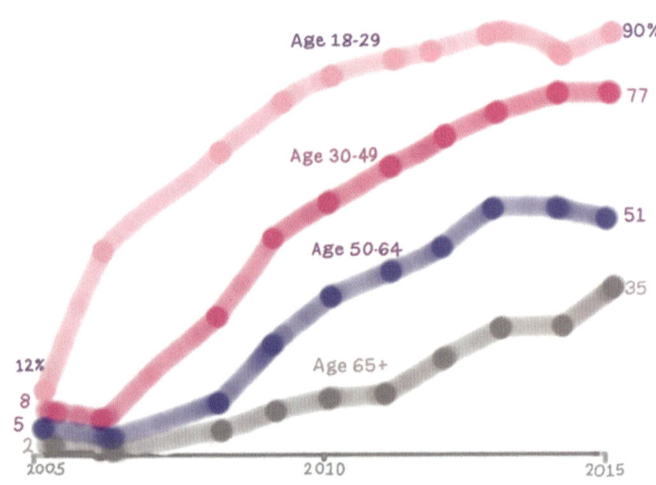

Source: Pew Research Center surveys, 2005-2006, 2008-2015. No data are available for 2007.

PEW RESEARCH CENTER

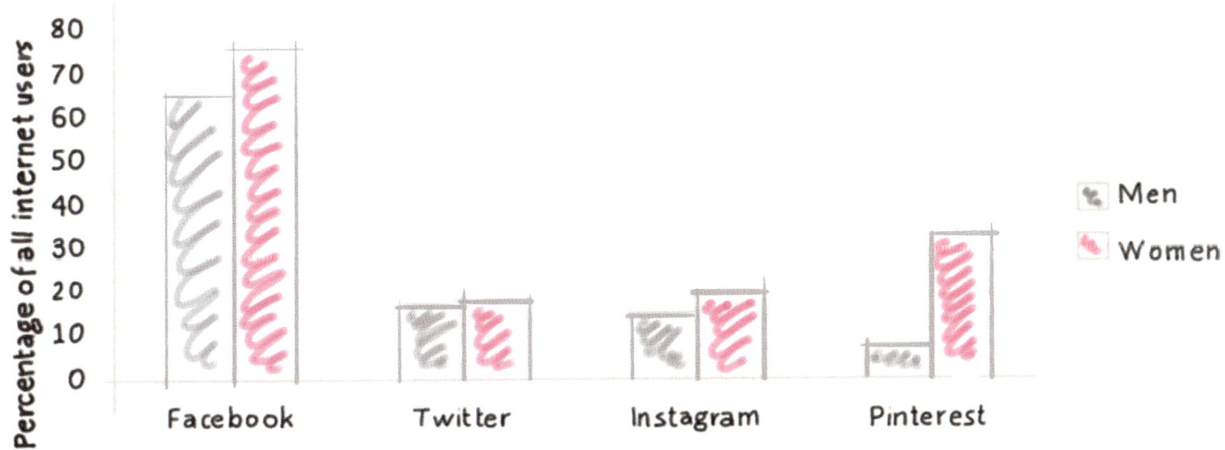

Think gender

Although similar percentages of men and women use social media sites, there are some fundamental differences in the way they use it, and which sites they use regularly.

For example, Pinterest is more popular with women than men, by a very long way.

If you're aiming at women, Pinterest is one of the best sites to attract them. Women spend lots of time on Pinterest. Men, not so much.

Think income

27% of internet users earning more than $75,000 (approx. £56,000) use Pinterest, compared to 15% of internet users who earn minimum wage or less.

This means better-off people (mostly women) are more likely to use Pinterest than people who earn less. If you've got very visual, well-priced work to sell, Pinterest and its users are just waiting for your goodies to drop into their 'basket'.

Of course, those people are probably also on Facebook, but that's a good thing. You get to reinforce your presence in two different places for those people.

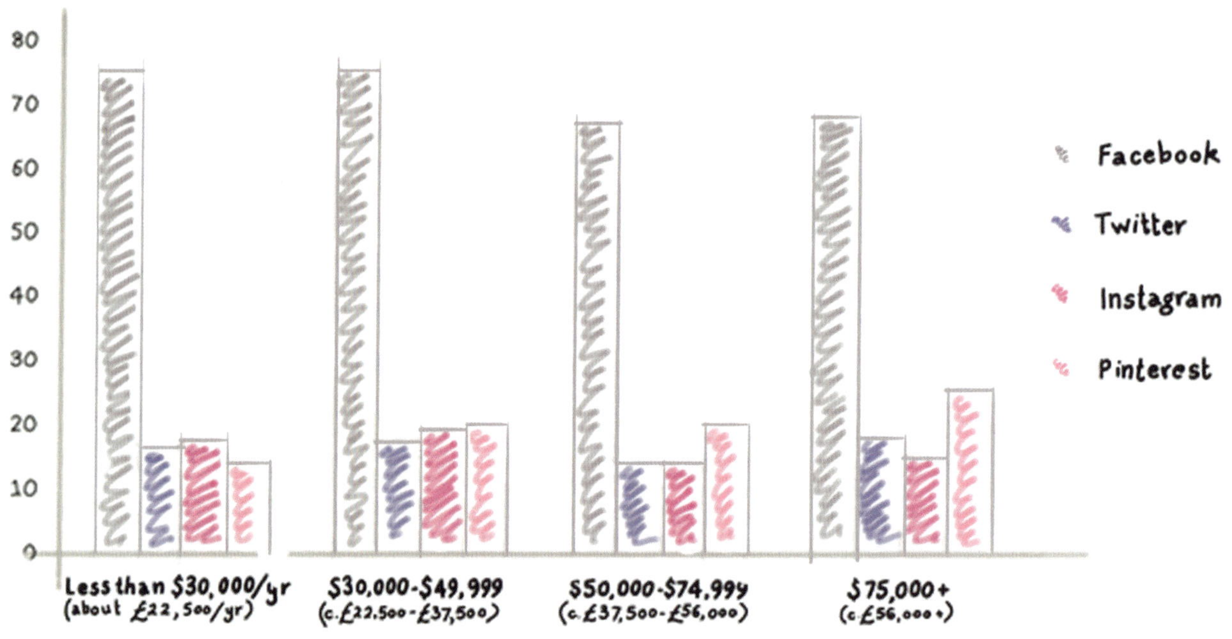

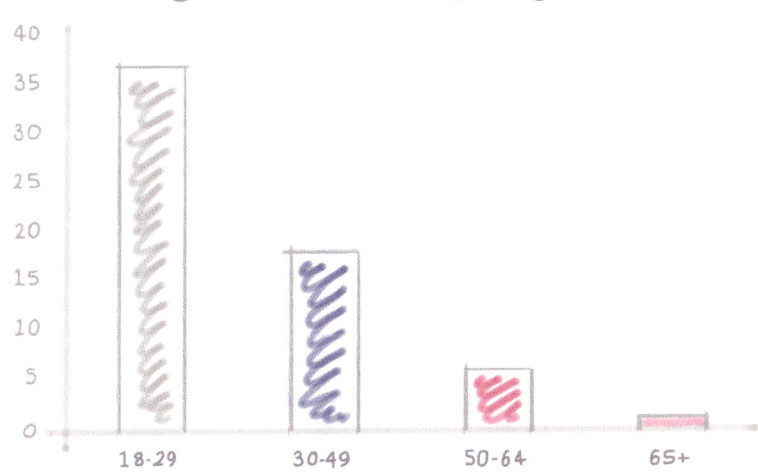

Think age

There are more young people on Instagram.

A lot more than any other age range.

Go for it, if younger adults are your market. Since Facebook bought Instagram, other age groups are using it more, but it's still top heavy with the yoof of today.

80% of all internet users between the ages of 18-49 use Facebook.

Facebook is the site most likely to catch everyone you want to sell your products to.

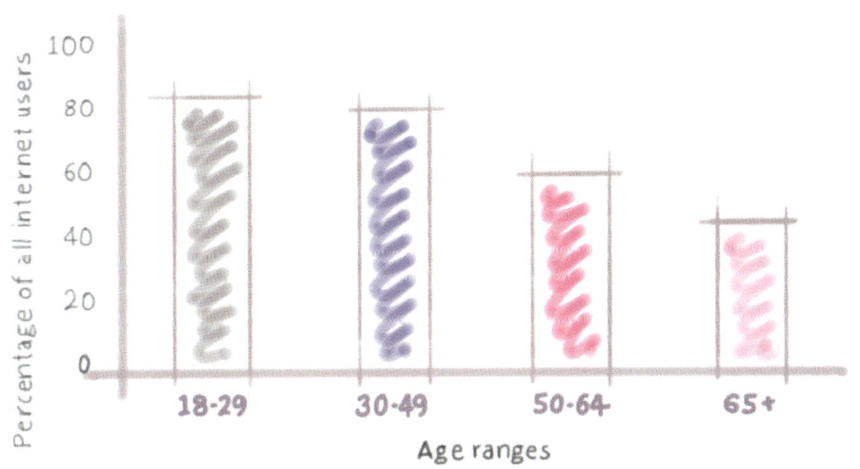

Find more potential customers

We advise you use two social media sites on a regular basis.

Why two?

There isn't enough time in the world to use more than two social media sites effectively for your marketing. Unless you have super powers, no kids, no partner or social life, and absolutely no desire to craft.

But if you only use one, you'll miss out on opportunities, and that would be crazy when you've worked so hard on your products.

Success on social media is somewhere between quantity and quality. It's not just about the number of posts you create, it's how well-targeted and interesting your posts are to your chosen audience. Two sites are enough for anyone who has some kind of life beyond work.

The danger is you end up automating a lot of posts, and that can lead to more impersonal-sounding marketing. Not good when you're trying to connect with customers.

If you think you're just too busy to maintain even two sites, you're probably right. Who isn't?!

But if you set them up now, you can play with them for a while and see what works better for you. You might find one goes dormant after a while, or you might switch between the two every so often. Maybe you'll find it all really easy to manage. Everyone's different.

The truth is Facebook is generally considered the best social media site to sell through, so we're going to ask you to select Facebook as your first 'choice' of social media site. It might seem a bit bossy, and you're within your rights to ignore this advice, but there are a bunch of good reasons for it! More on those in a moment.

Reach more people

Use two social media sites to make it easier for your potential customers to see your products. Show your products to more people and more people will buy them.

Which social media sites are you comfortable using?

We're focusing on these four, since they're the most popular social media sites out there:

- Facebook
- Twitter
- Instagram
- Pinterest

Upsides and downs of the social media world

Facebook

Facebook is number 1 for most people ...

- You'll get access to more people in almost any age or interest group.
- Business pages are simple and straightforward to set up.
- Facebook is very visual.
- Lots of free services, and the advertising cost is controllable.

... but it can be hard work.

- Facebook Shop section is super new in the UK, so not all features work yet.
- You may get bad reviews, fake bad reviews, or nasty comments.
- Facebook can suck up a lot of precious time.
- Facebook's algorithm changes can affect whether Facebook users can see your business page.

Twitter

Twitter never stops ...

- Free to use.
- Instant posts and messaging (this can be good and bad).
- Twitter makes it easy to search out your audience.

... but it can be like screaming in a crowd

- Getting attention can be frustrating.
- Twitter ads may not work unless you do dozens every time.

- Promoted tweets can be more expensive than Facebook ads.

Pinterest

Pinterest is great for visuals ...

- Gorgeous photos of your creations will attract attention on this site.
- If a Pinterest user interacts with a promoted pin, that person is 2-4 times more likely to buy the item. Those are good odds.

Pinterest is girly

It's not, of course, but Pinterest is about 85% female. It will be a good place to find female customers.

- If you spend more of your time on another site, Pinterest makes it easy to share pins to that site.
- You can use special 'keywords' to help your market find you really easily.

... but you can forget male customers.

- Pinterest isn't a great site to attract male users; a whopping 85% of current users are female.
- Users can skim Pinterest too easily, without reading at all. Just because they pin your posts doesn't mean they will buy.

Instagram

Instagram makes it easy to show off ...

- A visual site to show off your creativity.
- Easy system to make your photos look fab.
- Reach people with similar interests easily, using the search

... but it doesn't work for everyone.

- You can't sell directly through Instagram.
- Not everyone has a mobile phone that supports Instagram.
- Your photos have to look great, otherwise your biz won't look good.

What's special about Facebook?

Facebook is hands-down the best social media site for marketing.

It's geared up for selling, so you can find your target audience and get sales.

Most online people use it, with literally millions of people to sell to. And it's got space for words as well as images. Posts with pictures are more likely to be clicked on or looked at, worth remembering, even on your busiest days.

That's why we want you to make it easy on yourself and choose Facebook as one of your sites.

Later in the book, we explain how to create your own Facebook ads. Once you've mastered that, the promotional tools on the other sites will be much easier to use.

As far as your second main social media site goes, take your pick.

Direct selling: what is it, and can you do it on social media?

Direct selling is usually where you create a post that has a 'buy now' button.

That button enables the user to ... you got it: buy it now!

The customer doesn't have to leave the social media site to make the purchase, other than to log in to their payment app, and that keeps them on your Facebook page, so they can buy more stuff!

But here's the thing: on most social media sites, they either ask you not to do any direct selling, or the options they provide are currently limited.

For example:

- *You can set up a 'shop' section on Facebook, but the UK roll-out has only just begun, so not all the advertised features are available yet.*
- *Pinterest has what they call 'buyable pins', but they're only in the US right now, and won't be with the UK for a while longer.*
- *Instagram asks you to ignore direct sale posts, and encourages you to report them when you see any.*

So, what do you do about that?!

There are two main ways around this.

1. If you don't mind selling directly

On Facebook, Twitter, and Pinterest, you can create posts of your products and include the price and the product description.

Encourage people who are interested to comment below the picture, and when they do, point them towards messaging you directly with their order.

Help them with their buying decision by telling them what to do. If they want to buy, they'll follow the instructions!

That's a type of direct sale, just without the 'buy now' button.

2. If you prefer to sell only through your online shop or eBay

Use most of your social media posts to chat and make connections with your users, and with some of those posts and comments you can direct them (like a chatty signpost) to your shop site or products, as close to the 'buy now' button as possible. It's best if they can see the button when they arrive on that page.

Don't worry if you haven't got a shop yet - you will! Or you'll have somewhere to sell in any case.

We'll discuss 'directing users close to your goal' later in the book, but just keep it in mind for now.

So, which social media sites will you choose?

That was a lot of information, wasn't it?

Take your time, and think through the options. You don't have to make a decision in a hurry, but the idea is you stick with the chosen sites long term, so pick ones you like.

If you find after 3 or 6 months that one of your chosen sites isn't working that well, you can always ditch one and try another as a replacement. For example, you can get rid of Pinterest and use Twitter instead.

But before getting rid of a site, concentrate your efforts and have a really good go at the ones you pick. For example, you can try out different styles of post, to see if some work better than others.

Prep Task 3: Your social media sites

Get your notepad out, or just use the space provided here, and write down FACEBOOK as your number one choice. Decide which other site you want to use to promote your business.

- Twitter
- Instagram
- Pinterest

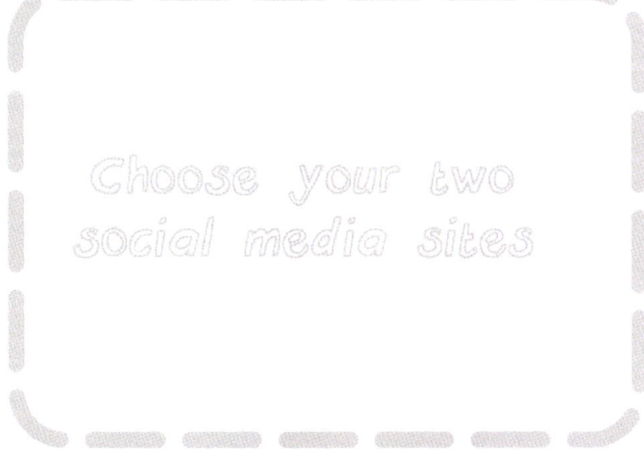

Well done!

You've now chosen to work with a suitable social media site alongside Facebook, to promote your burgeoning crafts business.

STEP 2
Set up your social media accounts and your shop

Now you've picked your two main sites, you'll want to get those up and running.

Social media websites are supposed to be super-easy to use, so that no-one can get stuck. But they still sometimes use unfamiliar language, so it's difficult to feel confident from the start.

We've all heard the horror stories about people who 'had a go' and ended up with terrifying advertising bills because they hadn't understood the terms. That's what we're going to avoid here!

As you'll know already, practice makes perfect, so we've provided detailed set-up instructions throughout this next section, with images from the sites.

Additionally, to be effective in marketing, there are certain pieces of information you'll need in your profile for each of the sites you decide to use, and for your online shops, so we've provided guidance on these.

Read on and find out how easily you can start selling your beautiful products!

TIP!

Read the parts from this section that are useful for you and skip the bits you don't need.

Facebook business pages

What's up with the Facebook business page?

Facebook is the undisputed king of social media.

A full 91% of people (in 2013) on social media use Facebook. That's why we're using it here as the number one social media site for marketing your crafts.

Luckily, because you're probably one of the 91%, you'll be in reasonably familiar territory. However, Facebook business pages can get a bit complicated, so we're sticking to the basics right now, and will cover other essential details later.

Facebook shop section

Facebook Shop is a section of your business page where you get to sell your products directly to customers.

At the time of writing in the UK it's running as a test version without all its advertised features, so although it might be useful for you when Facebook eventually rolls everything out, it's got limited value right now.

Get your free updates on Facebook Shop section at KerchingMarketingBooks.com/updates as the changes unfold.

If you live in North America, you'll already be able to access the fully functional Facebook Shop, so pop along to the above link and check out the information we have on that.

Let's get started!

Go to Facebook.com and log in as usual.

At the right-hand top corner of your screen, you'll see a tiny 'downwards' arrow. 1

Click the arrow.

You'll get a dropdown box with lots of options.

Click **Create Page**.

You're a brand, selling products

Click **Brand or Product.**

There are 6 choices of business page available, but when you're selling products, Brand or Product makes most sense as a category.

The Brand or Product box is the start of the process.

What is your business?

Click **Choose a category**. If you can't find an exact match to what you plan to offer, just pick **Product/Service** ❷ from the list.

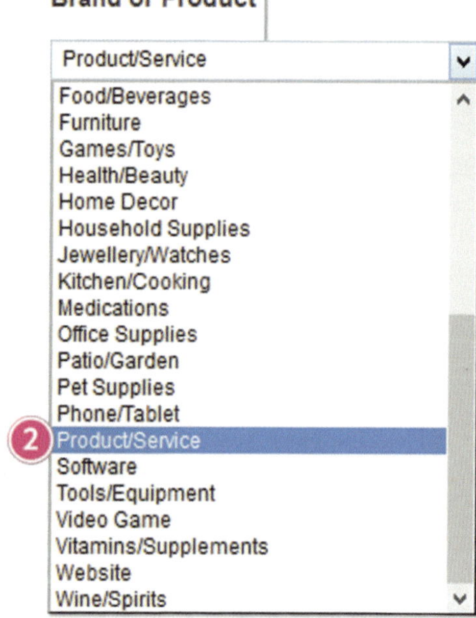

Next, type in the name of your new business.

Terms and conditions are important

It's good to read **Terms and Conditions (T&Cs)** when you are given the chance. It's smart to check up on T&Cs once in a while to make sure you haven't accidentally sold your soul. T&Cs are often full of legalese, so take half an hour to understand them properly. It might be worth doing one day, you never know.

Let's go

Click **Get Started**. You'll be taken directly to the **Set Up** page, on the **About** tab.

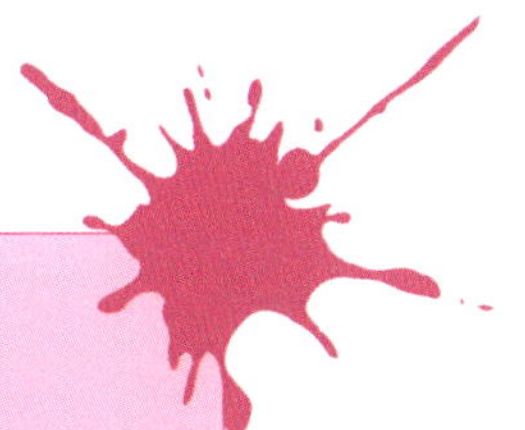

Work out the benefits

Benefits are hard to figure out sometimes, but they're a really important part of the marketing game.

Benefits aren't about how great your product is. They're about what your product does for your customers.

Your products improve lives

Benefits aren't about how great your product is. They're about what your product does for your customers.

Do you make hanging things and soft furnishings? Could you say your work brightens up homes and lives, and makes it really comfy at home?

Do you make beautiful, sparkly glasses for weddings and special occasions? Reassure your customers their tableware will be unique and memorable.

Do you make children's bows or hats? Your customers will love that no-one else's kid will be seen in the same smart gear.

Tell the world what you do, in just a few words.

We've typed in some text to give you an idea of what you could include in your short description. 3

You only have 155 characters, including spaces - just a few more than for a tweet - so it can be a challenge to get everything in. You'll manage it though! If you ever get stuck with this sort of thing, just take a breather and come back to it later.

It's best if you mention the things you make the most often and well, and finish off with something about why the customer will love your makes. Go for a professional, but confident tone.

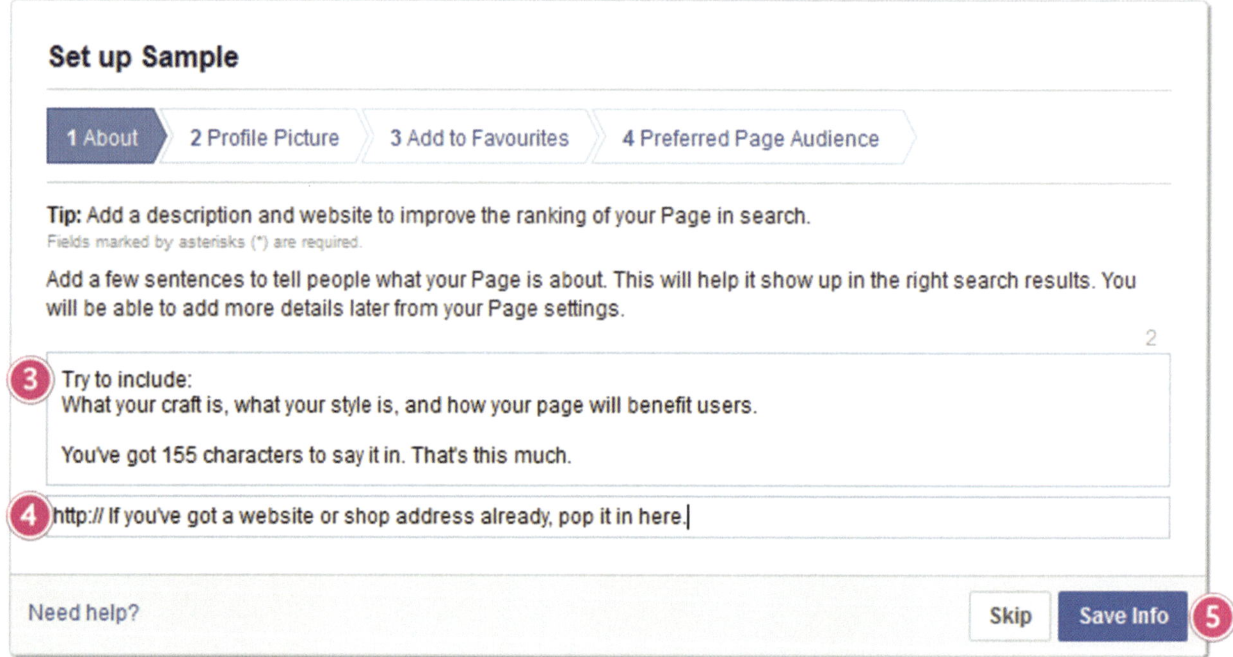

Advertise your website address

If you have a website or have already set up your shop, pop that address in the website box. 4

Click **Save info.** 5

The page will move to the next 'tab', **Profile Picture**.

Put a profile picture on your page.

Click **Upload from computer** and follow the usual instructions for putting a picture on Facebook.

Choose one of your best makes if it's easy to see in the picture. Something distinctive is best.

Otherwise, get yourself a logo. If you're no good with fancy graphics software like Adobe Photoshop or Gimp, there are other options: with websites like PeoplePerHour.com and Fiverr.com, you can get something nice made quickly and cheaply.

Give it a few seconds to load - the image will appear in the box on the left.

Click **Save Photo.**

Favourite your page

You'll be taken to the next tab, Add to Favourites.

Get your page into your Favourites, so it shows up on the left column of your screen on your Facebook homepage.

Your page name will appear below the central box, so click the green **Add to Favourites** button.

Take aim at your audience

Click on **Preferred Page Audience**.

This tab is the important one.

Now flip out your notebook from earlier, or go back through this book, and look at the notes you made about your audience.

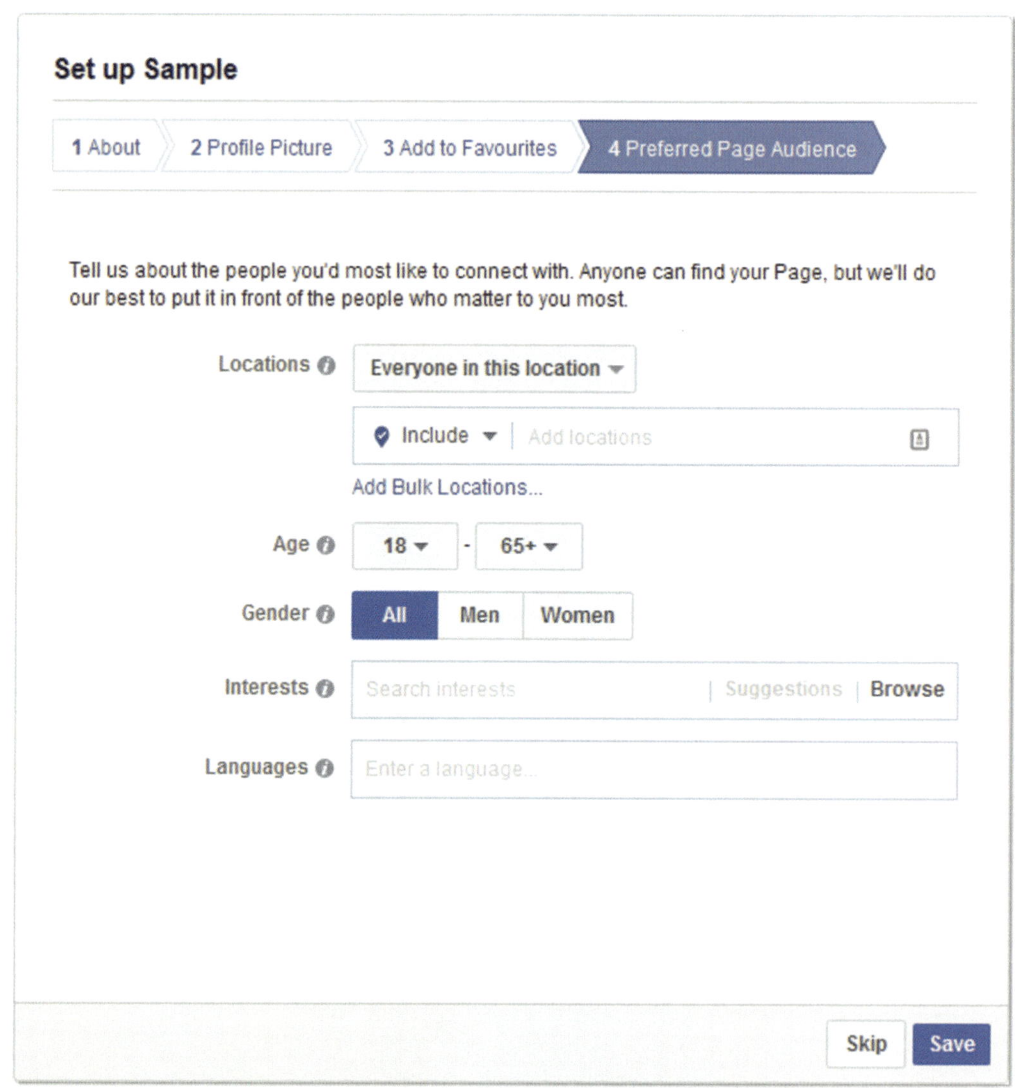

How old they are, their gender, and all those other things are important.

Postage and profit

The cost of postage may increase your international customers' overall spend too much, so it could be easier and more profitable to aim for UK customers to start with.

You'll also need to think about location. Do you want to sell in the UK only, or would you like to try for an American or European market too? If you want a wider audience, and you don't mind posting your sales internationally, choose more than one country to target. It's totally up to you.

These **Preferred Page Audience** settings will help you choose a wide range of people who may be interested in your crafts and skills.

Where are your potential customers?

Click **Everyone in this location** and make sure the first option is selected with a small check-mark/tick.

Click in the box to the right of **Include** and start typing **United Kingdom** if that's where you intend to sell your work. Select it when it appears, and it will turn bold above the word **Include.**

If you only want to sell to the UK, you don't need to add any others.

If you love the idea of posting to other countries, type their names next to **Include** and select them as they appear.

How old will your customers be?

Choose the age range of your audience. Leave it as is if you want to aim at all adults between 18-65 years of age, but if you'd prefer to make it a little narrower, that's cool. For example, university students might be 18-45+.

What gender do your customers identify as?

Choose which gender you want to target, but if your products are great for everyone, go ahead and click on All.

What will your customers be interested in?

Click inside the **Search interests** box.

A dropdown box will appear, so choose **Hobbies and activities.** 6

Select **Arts and music.** 7

That will give you a new list, so you can then choose **Crafts.** 8

It's kinda nice to look at the box that appears on the right-hand side of the

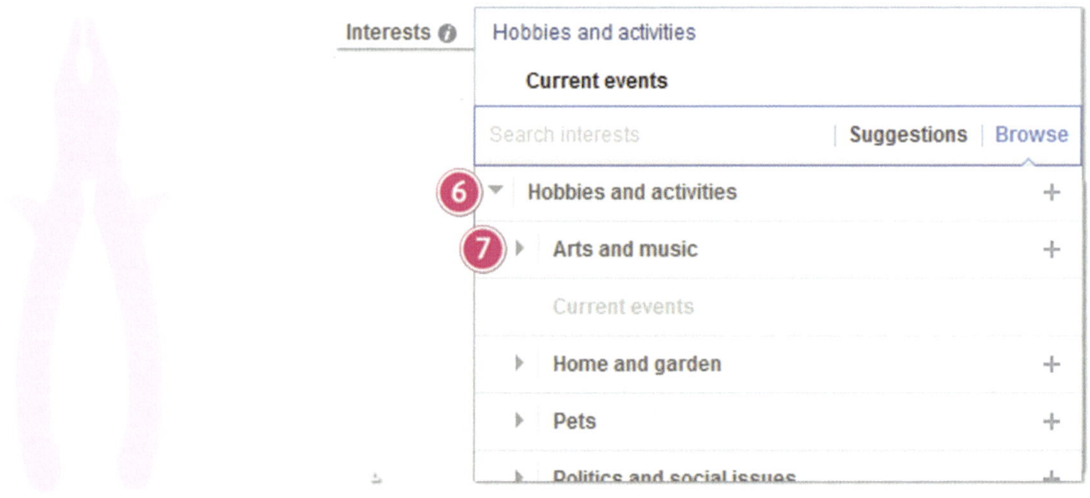

screen as you run your mouse over the list. The box shows you how many people have said they are 'interested' in Crafts.

Over 100 million people at the time of writing. There's a lot of people out there. A lot of potential opportunity.

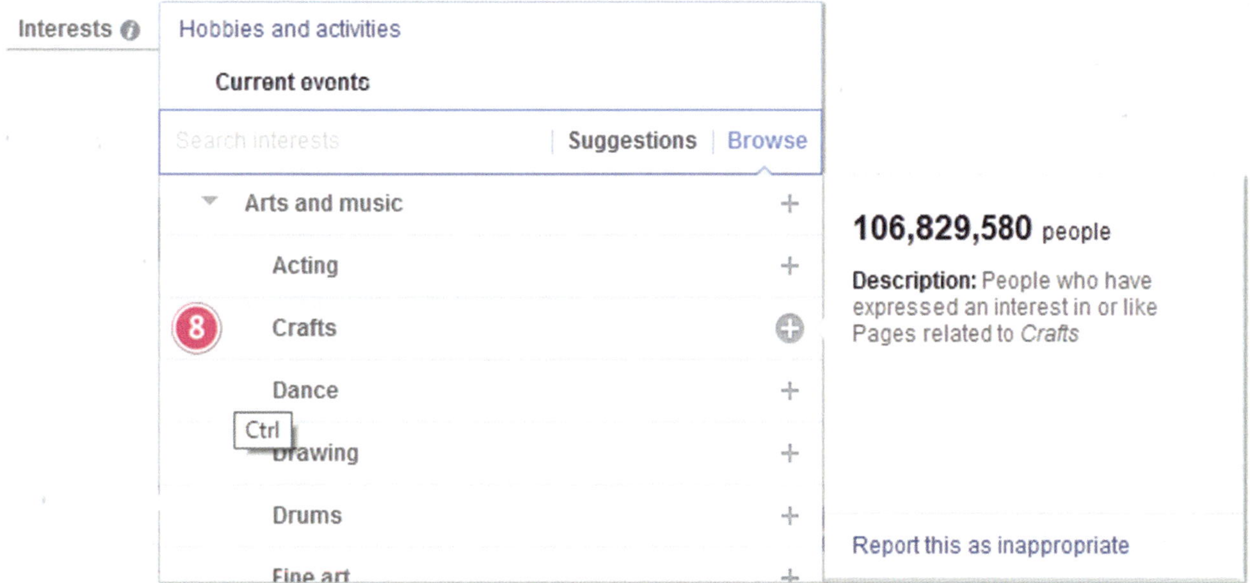

You should now see this:

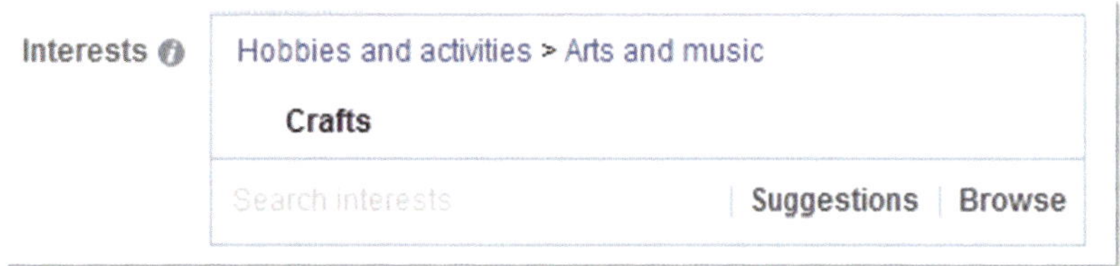

Specify your craft

Click in the **Search interests** box. 9

A new dropdown list will give you lots of different choices of craft type to pick, so you should pick something closely related to what you do.

Again, the box on the right shows you how many millions of people are interested in the specific craft you do.

You can choose more than one if you are going to offer more than one type of craftwork for sale.

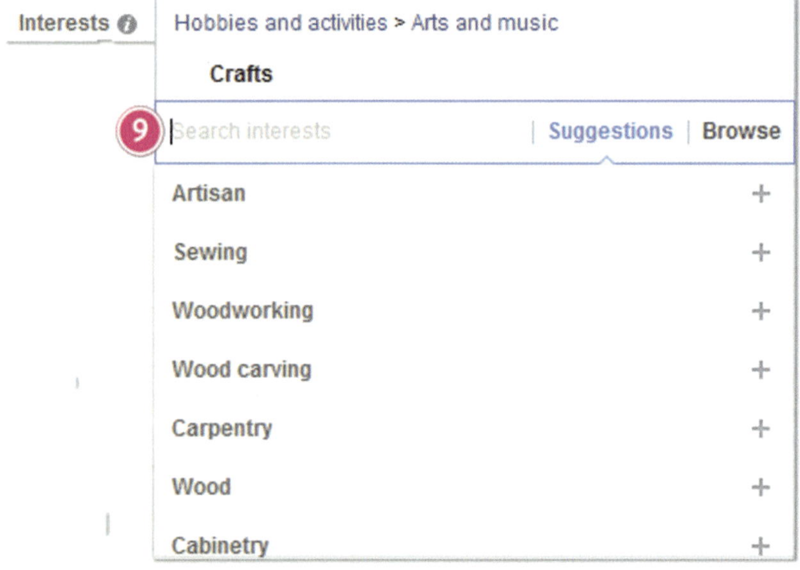

Pick your Language

Click in the box and start typing the name of your language.

You can have as many as you want, but it's best if you can speak and understand those languages!

Now you've finished the page, click **Save.** The next page you see will look something like this:

Upload your cover photo

Click on the **camera icon** at the top left of the grey cover and follow the instructions. Choose a photo to represent you and the things you make, or something to give viewers a good idea of what you're about.

You did it!

As you can see, the page functions pretty much the same way as your normal Facebook profile. You create posts in the usual way, and you can add photos and videos just the same.

The main differences are in what you post - your content - and the big 'Boost Post' button under each post, but we'll deal with both those things later.

For now, why don't you take some time to get to know your new page, or go ahead and immediately set up your second social media account?

Twitter for business

How does Twitter work for marketing?

Twitter isn't for everyone, but it's a good way to get a sweeping overview of the headlines of people's lives and world events, as long as you choose to follow people you're genuinely interested in.

When it comes to marketing, that headline thing applies to the work you do. You might post a tweet about your latest work, but if you stick a picture on it, you're more likely to get people clicking on it to see what it is. Twitter doesn't usually show the whole picture unless tweets are clicked on, so curious people will click.

Pictures work wonders. Don't underestimate them; use the best ones you have for your marketing. You can't use pictures of other people's work unless you have a legal arrangement with them, and it's not a good idea to use commercial images to 'give an idea' of the sort of thing you do. That can sometimes mislead the audience.

The great thing about Twitter is this: lots of people follow back. So if you follow someone, there's a reasonably high chance they will follow you back. Whether they stick around depends on whether you tweet about things they're interested in. If they disappear, that doesn't matter - they weren't your audience anyway.

Your potential customers will stay with you, and will gradually grow in number, as long as you keep your focus on tweeting about your craft, your materials, your successes, and sometimes your products.

Get cracking on Twitter!

If you never used Twitter before

If you don't already belong to Twitter, go to Twitter.com right now!

In the top right-hand of your screen you should see this:

Click **Sign up.** ① 

If you already have a Twitter account

If you already use Twitter, **log out.**

To log out, go to your profile picture at the right-hand top edge of your screen ② and click it.

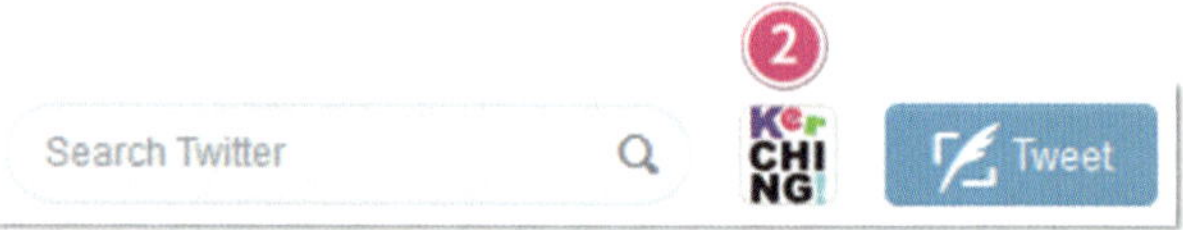

You'll get a dropdown box with log out listed at the bottom.

Click **log out.**

Look to the top right-hand corner of your screen again.

You should see this: ③

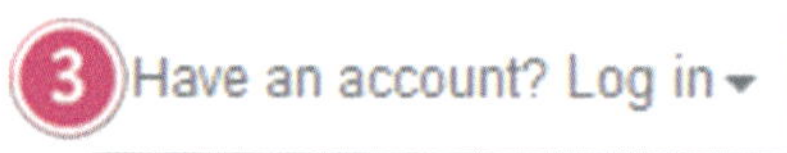

Click it. This log-in box gives you a **Sign up** option, so go ahead, hit that button.

Sign up to Twitter

Whether you've used Twitter before, or you had to log out, you should now see a box that looks like this:

Click **Sign up.** 4

Fill out your name, your email address, and the password you want to use.

Click **Sign up** (again).

If you have no email address, just type in your mobile number, and Twitter will send you a confirmation text with a code for you to fill out on the next screen.

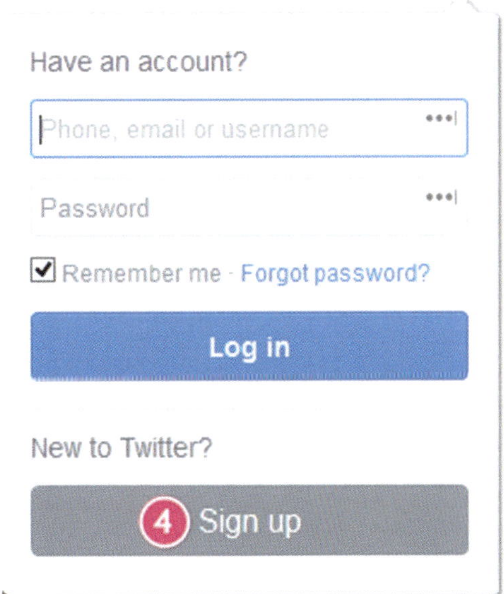

Really Important!

If you already belong to Twitter under your usual email address, you'll need to create a new email account. You can do this for free with any web-based email provider, such as **Gmail**, **Hotmail**, or **Outlook**.

Confirm you're a real person

Fill out your telephone number and click **Next.**

Type in a username that reflects your business. Something that hints at what you do or the style you do it in.

Click **Next.**

Get your logo up there

Click on the **camera icon** and upload your logo or a suitable picture for your profile picture.

Click **Continue.**

After this you'll be bombarded by Twitter trying to get you to follow random celebrities. It's up to you if you do so, or if you prefer to leave your page completely blank from the get-go.

If you haven't used Twitter before, following recommended accounts may help you learn how it works. Otherwise, there's no real need.

Who to follow, and why

Twitter can get chaotic pretty quickly, and it's difficult - and sometimes expensive - to organise it after it becomes crazy. For your business account you can work a couple of simple systems:

- Always follow back, especially if the person's profile mentions craft or shopping or supporting small business.
- Track down other people interested in your craft and follow them.

Following back

When someone follows you, open up the notification or their profile, and follow them. Following someone back is like a mark of respect. It's a nod in their direction to say 'thanks'. It's just polite, and you don't have to stay their follower if you find their tweets aren't relevant to your mission.

Every follower could be a potential customer under the right circumstances, so you want the opportunity for a two-way chat as quickly as possible.

Tracking down potential customers

If you follow people who are interested in your craft, there's a strong chance they'll follow you back. So where do you find these people?

Twitter's search function is actually pretty good. If you type the name of your craft into the search box, you'll pull a lot of tweets about it.

You can then go through the tweeters' profiles and choose if you think they're worth following. Or just follow them. You can unfollow if they annoy you.

If you do this more than once, there'll be a few new people to follow each time. If you forget about it forever, it doesn't matter; doing it once will get you following people on Twitter.

A good percentage of those tweeters will follow you back, so this is a way to pick up followers and reach more people.

If they decide to follow you, they may also occasionally retweet your posts. If that happens, your post goes out to their followers, and increases your reach even further.

Using the Twitter Dashboard for your business

The Twitter Dashboard is a really new addition to using Twitter for business, and long term, it could be pretty useful to you if you've decided to use Twitter as your second social media account.

The most important use of it for now will be its scheduling tool, where you get to put up posts in advance, using the calendar provided. It's fiddly but gives you a chance to plan out a few posts a few days at a time.

Follow these instructions to start using Twitter for business with the new Twitter Dashboard.

Log in to Twitter.com under your business account you set up earlier.

Go to dashboard.twitter.com.

Click the large blue button in the centre of the screen: **Try Twitter Dashboard**.

You'll land on a page that looks like this:

Choose **Online Business**, and select **One person** in the dropdown box at the bottom of the screen.

Click **Next.**

You'll now see your business Twitter account on the screen, and it probably looks pretty bare unless you've already been tweeting from it for some time.

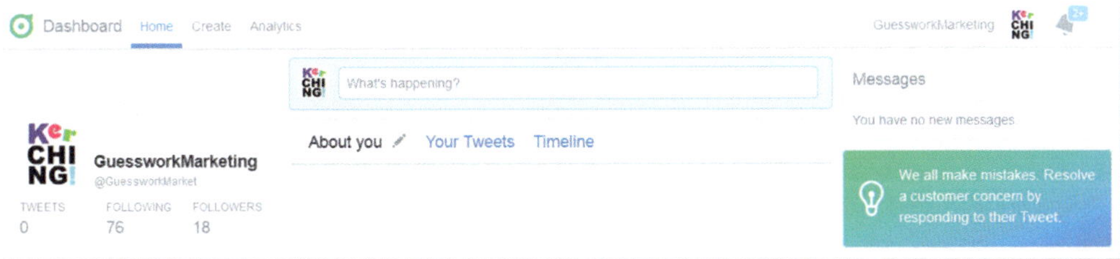

At the top left of the screen, you should see this menu:

Click **Create.**

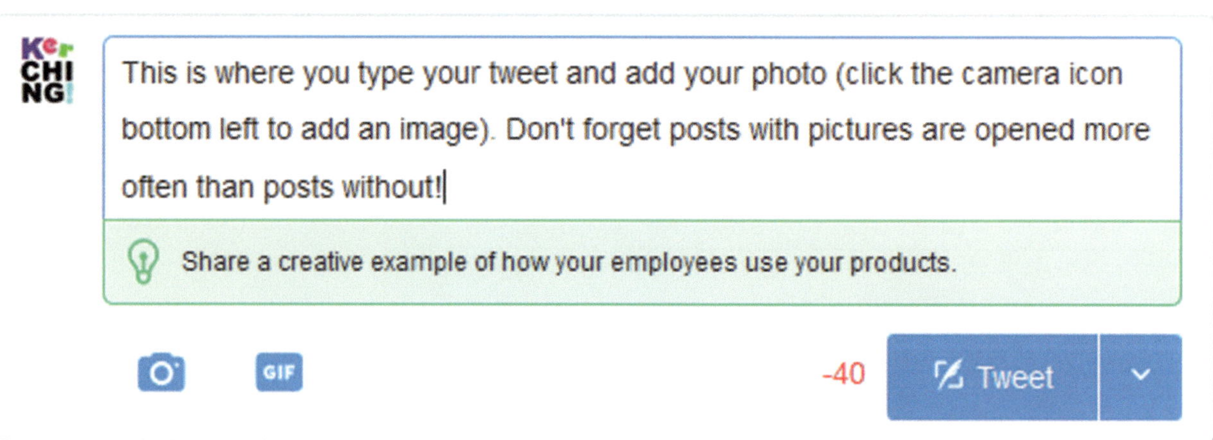
KerCHING!
This is where you type your tweet and add your photo (click the camera icon bottom left to add an image). Don't forget posts with pictures are opened more often than posts without!
Share a creative example of how your employees use your products.
GIF
-40
Tweet

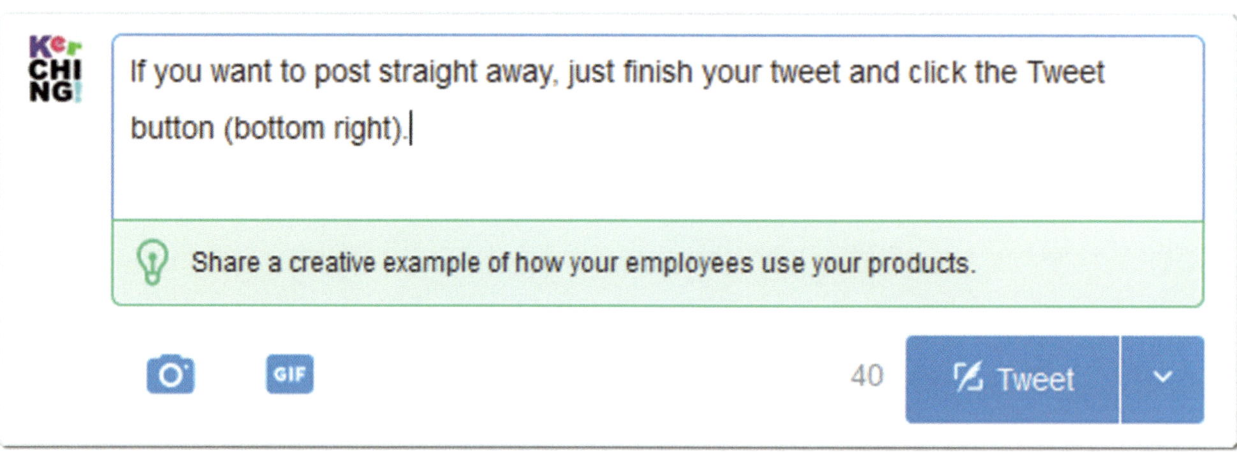
KerCHING!
If you want to post straight away, just finish your tweet and click the Tweet button (bottom right).
Share a creative example of how your employees use your products.
GIF
40
Tweet

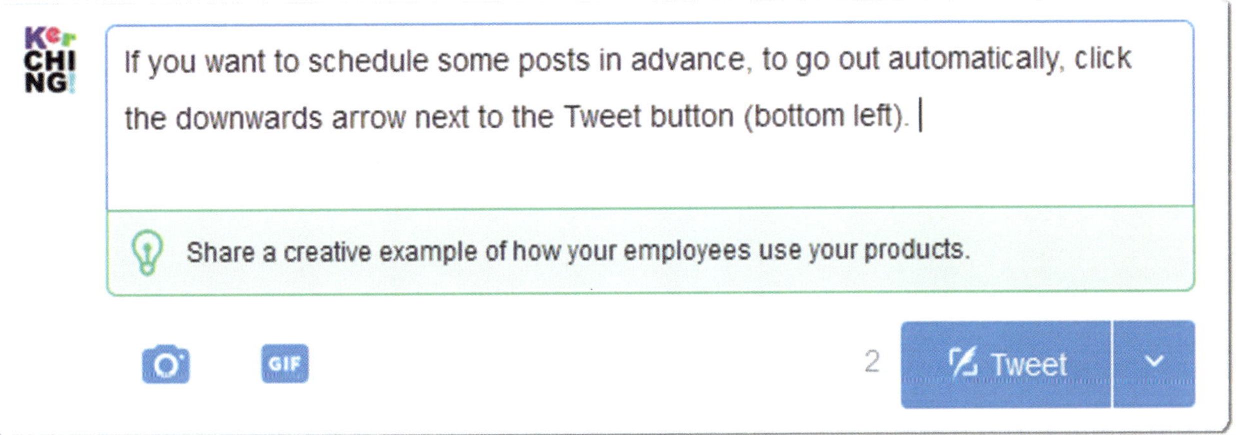

So if you want to schedule a few posts in advance, click the downwards arrow on the right of the Tweet button, and you'll now see this on your screen:

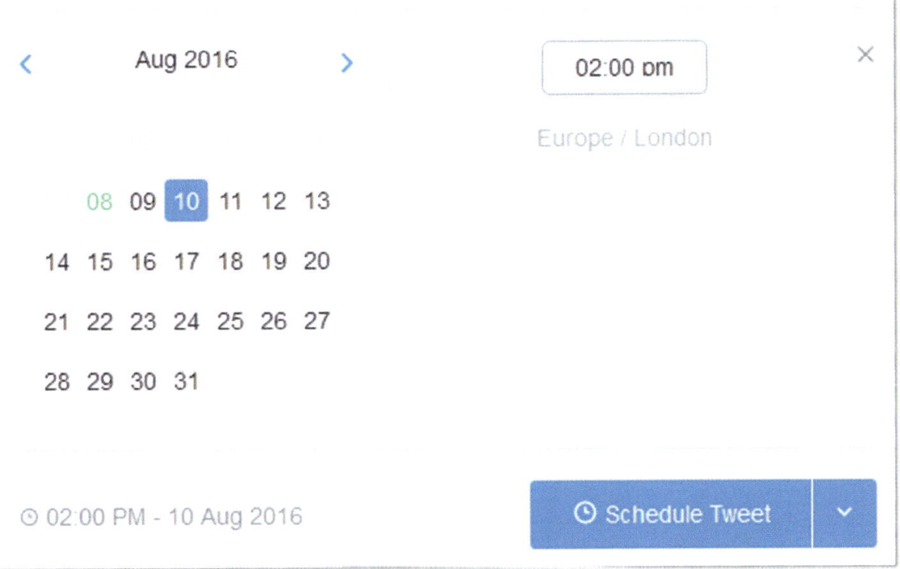

Select a date and a time, and hit the big blue button.

The **Queue** list below will show each tweet you have scheduled, including the set time and date you chose.

If you want to check all your queued tweets, or if you're trying to send one out for every hour and want to see if there's a gap in the schedule anywhere, click **Show calendar.**

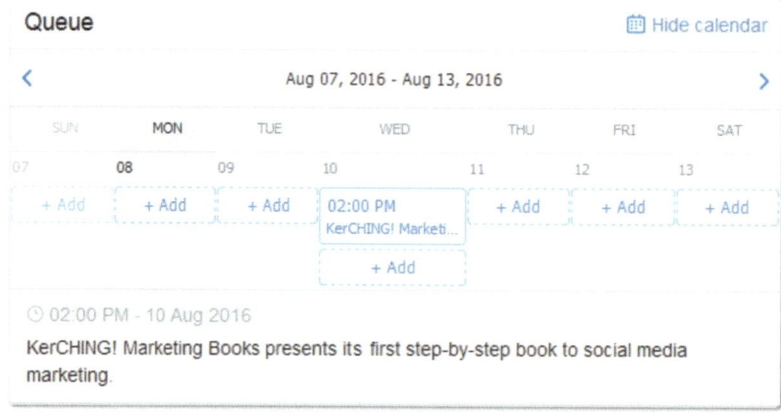

A brief word about Twitter analytics

There's also an Analytics section in your Twitter dashboard. This might become pretty useful to you after you've got the hang of Facebook analytics (details in Step 3), but at this stage we suggest just keeping an occasional eye on the Analytics tab, especially if you're wondering how well your individual posts are doing.

As you begin to understand the Facebook analytics better, the Twitter ones will also make more sense and over time you'll be able to tweak your tweets to get the maximum interest and attention from your followers.

Don't worry about analytics

There are hundreds of marketing tricks designed to make it easier to sell products, but all you really need to know from the start is here in this book. With analytics, you'll learn as you earn.

It's really interesting looking at how each different post did, and what you did right or wrong; just have a poke around. You'll soon figure out if it's going to help or hinder you, but don't spend money until you're sure you know what you're getting.

Twitter: sorted!

Twitter is a hive of marketing activity. Professional marketers can spend over 6 hours a day publishing promotional tweets - the more time you spend, the better your results will be.

Stay realistic, especially if you have a family, a job, and a real life to get on with.

In real life terms, 5 tweets per day should be enough to keep you afloat on Twitter, and may gain you followers easily. Fewer than 5, and your presence may not be enough to be noticed. Twitter is a crowd, so tweets move quickly across screens. More than 5 is better, but it's totally up to you.

You could create a series of tweets ahead of time, but how you do that is up to you. If you've got a smartphone, a Memo or Notes app can be handy. Otherwise use your diary or a piece of paper on a noticeboard, or every time you think of a tweet, pop it in a memo. Just subjects and ideas will do.

If you ever find you're struggling for inspiration (on the fourth and fifth tweets of the day, maybe), just get out your notes and use your ideas. That's what they're for!

Pinterest business account

What's in a pin?

Pinterest is a lovely, visual medium; something you can scroll through for hours.

Jewellery, crafts, ideas, tutorials ... it's a rich environment for handmade crafts.

Pinterest focuses on the idea of 'discovery'. All those pictures give people the chance to find new things. When they discover your products or shop, you want to give them new things to see.

Keeping your boards fresh, and your pins useful or interesting is a key part of maintaining your site. You can keep it relevant by making pins about different aspects of your craft, or related interests like paint and colours.

Also, women outnumber men on Pinterest. So there's lots of opportunity for female customers, but men who use Pinterest may be a narrower market.

Start pinning!

If you never used Pinterest before

Go to **Pinterest.com.**

If you're already a Pinterest user

If you're already a user on Pinterest, you'll need to **log out**.

Click the button with the little man in the top right of your screen.

It'll take you to your profile page.

Click the button with the three round dots:

Select **Log out** from the dropdown list.

You'll be taken to the standard **Sign up** screen but *you're not going to use it yet.* See over the page.

All users join as a business

Ignore the form on the right. Click the Businesses 1 link at the bottom of the screen.

Click the big red button **Join as a business**. The link underneath asks if you'd like to convert your personal account to your businesss one. It's up to you, but I prefer the separation of my public and private personas. The next screen will be the **Create a Business Account** form.

Create a new account

Fill out your **email address**, and create a **password** for your new account.

You'll have to confirm your email address later by clicking on a link in an email sent to you by Pinterest, but you don't have to go do that right away.

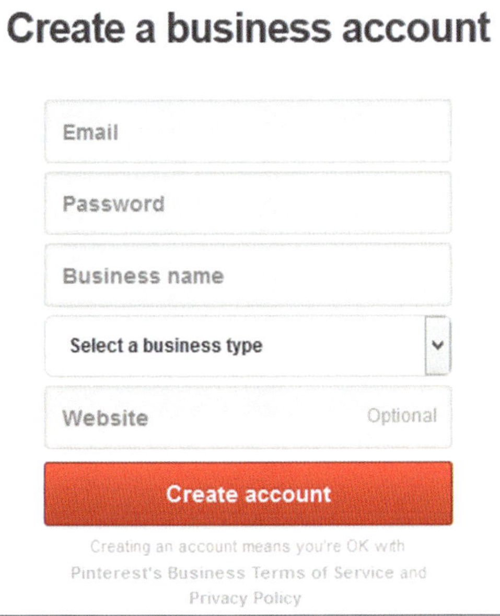

Enter your website address

If you already have a website, or an online shop address, type that into the **Website** box. If you don't have either of those things just yet, don't worry about it. Pinterest want to know your website address so they can track your traffic, but if you're not going to use the statistics much, it won't really matter.

Select a business type from the dropdown list.

Choosing the right business type

It won't be a matter of life or death to pick the 'correct' business type for your Pinterest account, but the choices you can pick from include:

- Professional
- Brand
- Retailer
- Local business

Any of these might work for you, but pick one you feel will work best with your new business.

Create your Pinterest account

Click **Create account**.

Select 5 topics you want to see in your feed. You can search for crafts, sewing, and other related topics in the search box at the top of the screen.

Click **Done**.

Agree to get the Pinterest browser button if you think that will be useful, otherwise click Skip (located just below the big red button at the bottom of the screen). Pinterest will ask you again if you skip, so just skip, or go back and agree to it if you have changed your mind.

Give Pinterest a few moments to configure everything for your page, and you will then be taken to your feed.

Sort out your settings straight away

Click on your tiny profile picture at the top right-hand corner of your screen.

A dropdown list will appear.

Select **Settings**.

You should now be on a page called **Business account basics**.

Make your pins public

Scan the list, and look for **Search privacy** (see image). It asks you if you want to

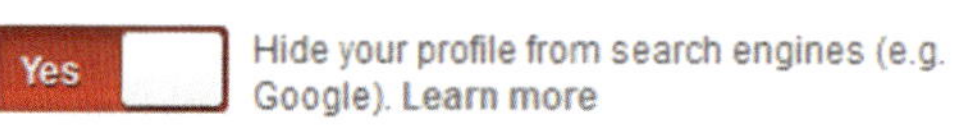

hide your profile from search engines. If you do, and you click the switch to show 'yes', your pages will stop showing up in public. That's not a good thing for a business account, especially when you're selling.

If you want search engines (and therefore potential customers) to find your crafting pins and pages easily, click the switch so it shows a light grey **No** slider like this:

Scroll down the page, to a section called **Profile.**

Get your picture up

Click **Change picture**, and follow the usual instructions to upload your profile picture. It can be your Facebook profile picture, a logo, or you can offer up a different image for your Pinterest crowd.

Create your username

Make your username as cool as you like. It has to be between 3 and 15 letters long, and you can't use any fancy punctuation like !. It's best if usernames are memorable, so keep it simple!

Pinterest bio

Under **Username**, you'll find a box labelled **About you**. Copy and paste your Facebook page description into this, or come up with a new original description for your business.

Help local people find you

Type in your **location** if you want. This helps people who live near you find your work more easily.

Set your notifications

Scroll further down the page. You'll come to a section called **Notifications.** Set these functions so they bother you the least, but remember: they can be useful.

It won't be too important to be notified by Pinterest on every movement other people make, but you don't want to miss the chance to respond to someone who comments on your pins or repins them. Social media marketing is two-way communication between you and your potential customers, so responding to comments is crucial.

It's up to you if you choose **Only people you follow**, or **Get notifications from everyone**. The first may mean you miss out on strangers commenting and repinning; the second could have your email inbox heaving with notifications, or your phone buzzing constantly.

If you don't want any notifications, click the sliders for **By email** and **On your desktop**, so they become a grey **No**.

If you have a smartphone, **On your phone** will let you edit the 'push notifications' if you need.

> ### Two-way communication
>
> Social media marketing is two-way communication between you and your potential customers, so responding to comments is crucial.

When you've messed on with all your settings, don't forget to click the all-important **Save settings** button!

Using other social networks alongside Pinterest.

You can't currently connect your Facebook business page directly to your Pinterest business account.

However, you can log in with Facebook, but only if you don't have another Pinterest account linked with your personal Facebook account.

If you have already connected your Facebook profile to a personal Pinterest account, you won't be able to log into your Pinterest business account using Facebook unless you disconnect it from your personal account.

Disconnect your Facebook profile from your personal Pinterest account

If this is the case for you, and you really want to connect Facebook with your Pinterest business account, go to your personal Pinterest profile, select the **bolt button** and scroll down the settings to **Social networks**. Under **Log in with Facebook**, click the slider till it shows a grey **No**.

Tips and Troubleshooting
You cannot connect your business's Facebook account/page. We currently only support personal Facebook accounts.

You can then log in to your business account, go to your settings the exact same way, and click the same slider till it shows a red and white **Yes**.

Even though your Facebook business account isn't connected directly to your Pinterest business account, you can still post on your Facebook business wall. Every time you share a pin to Facebook, click on the dropdown box **Share on your own timeline**. Select **Share on a page you manage** and click on your business page.

Whenever you post something you think will work on Facebook, share it to Facebook this way.

Create your first Pinterest board

One more thing: when you've set up your account the way you like it, you'll be asked if you want to create a board.

Boards are what you fix your pins to, so you'll need at least a couple of different boards to begin with, just to organise your pins.

Follow the instructions to create your board.

Creating pins

On Pinterest

When you notice a pin you really like from someone else's boards, just roll your mouse over it till you see this pin icon:

Click it, and save it into one of your boards. If you don't have a board that seems relevant but you still want to save the pin, just click **Create new board** and follow the instructions.

On the web

You can create pins by visiting a site of interest and pressing the Pinterest browser button. Follow the brief instructions, and voilà, you will have created a pin from around the web.

On your device

In the top right-hand of your screen, near your profile picture, you'll find a round, grey icon, with a + in the centre.

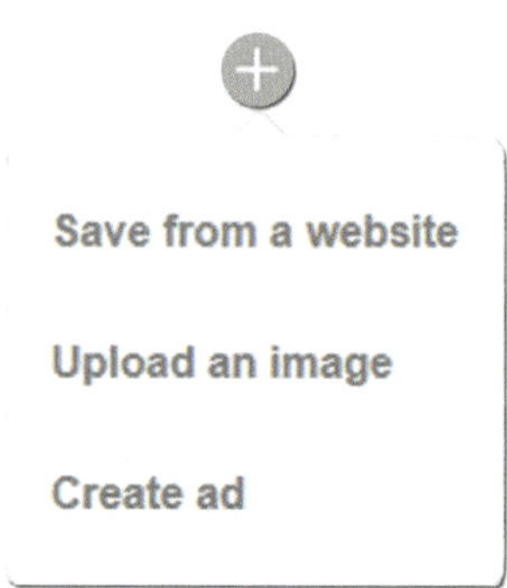

Click the icon, and select **Upload an image**.

Choose an image, wait for it to upload, then write something inspiring, useful or informative, and totally, totally relevant, in the box provided under the photo.

Select an existing board, or create a new one, and click **Save**.

Promoting pins

Because you're a business, every time you pin something, Pinterest will ask you if you want to promote that pin.

Promotional post settings are similar across the different sites, so once you've got the hang of one, you'll be better able to set out with the others. This book is focused on Facebook, since it's the most popular social media site by a long way.

We'll introduce you later to Facebook promoted posts. When you've had a play with those, you'll be in a better position to test out promoted posts on other sites.

Pinterest is open for business!

Pinterest is a great place for engagement. It's about making links with other people via the things they're interested in. You can pin your own tutorials, your own work, and images that inspire you.

You can also pin inspiration you find across the Internet, and spread the word about other people's work.

There's nothing to be lost in talking about and admiring other people's work. In doing so you become a trustworthy source of information, and people come back to those sources time and again.

Instagram for business

Lovely, easy photography

Instagram creates perfectly square photographs, which makes them easy to compose.

You can centre the subject or shoot it on an angle, and it's easy to make it look really nice.

Filters are an added feature of Instagram, so you can alter colour, contrast, and mess on with the images until they look super-arty ... However, there is a BIG caveat. Your potential customers need to see your work in normal light. When you sell online, you're selling 'as seen', but that means you have to show your product as seen by the naked eye.

Enjoy the filters, but don't rely on Instagram for your product shots. You'll need better quality photos for your shop.

Instagram is a very pretty form of bait. You can use it to lure in customers, and your beautiful filtered, well-balanced and composed photos will catch their attention. After that, you can show them your product shots.

Get snapping on Instagram

If you already use Instagram

If you already have an account with Instagram, **log out**.

It's tricky to find Instagram's log out function, so follow these instructions carefully so you don't have to Google it.

Go to **Instagram.com**.

Click on the little person icon at the top right-hand of your screen:

This will take you to your main page. You'll be able to see lots of your recent photos there.

Next to your name you will see this:

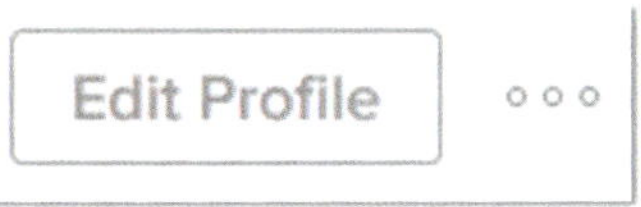

Click those three little dots, and you'll be asked if you want to **log out.**

Go for it.

When you get back to the Instagram.com page, you'll see a suggestion to log in as your usual account, but underneath that, it'll ask you if you want to **Switch accounts.** Yes you do.

For new and old Instagram users

Make sure you're on Instagram.com, logged out. You'll be shown a login screen, but right at the bottom there's a Sign up link. Click it.

Sign up to Instagram

Type in your email address, the name of your business, and your username. Make up a password and click **Sign up**.

App invitation

Accept or ignore the app invitation - it's up to you. The Instagram app is the easiest way to get your pictures loaded to your account, but it's only for smartphones, so if your phone is older and more basic, you won't be able to use the app.

Get your face or your logo on Instagram

Add a **profile photo**. Instagram will only let you upload a standard JPG image, so if your profile picture is a PNG or any other type of image, you won't be able to find it. If you do manage to select an image that isn't a JPG, Instagram will pretend to do the upload, but really it won't do anything!

Choose a profile picture Instagram can see and upload it.

Your Instagram bio

Click on the little person icon again in the top-right of your screen,

and this time, when you see Edit Profile, click it (instead of the three dots).

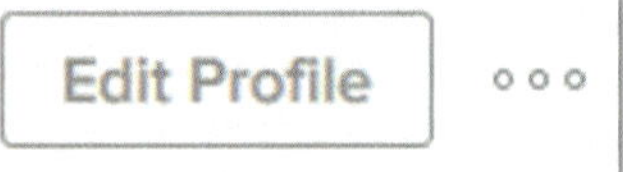

You can either copy your Facebook short description, and pop it into the Bio box in your Instagram profile, or you can write a nice new one. Once again, it's up to you; it's your time and effort.

Fill out any other bits you think are important on Instagram's profile, and when you've finished, click **Submit.**

Instagram your crafts!

Give yourself a slap on the back and break open something delicious to celebrate! You've got yourself an Instagram business account, and if you've downloaded the app to your smartphone, you'll be able to share with the world the daily trials and tribulations of your craftiness as much or as little as you like.

It's a downer you can't watermark or otherwise sign your Instagram pictures, but the upside is that loading a unique photo onto Instagram will only take a minute of your time.

In addition, Instagram belongs to Facebook, so you can easily connect those two accounts and have them work together. For example, when you upload a new picture to Instagram, you can set it to publish on Facebook simultaneously.

Choose your own online shop

You don't need a website to have an online shop.

In fact, you really don't need a shop to sell online. That's where Facebook Shop section will come in eventually, when it rolls out fully. Besides, there are plenty of sellers who have just been using business pages and the Buy and Sell groups and doing just fine.

However, there are also plenty of online shop options available that won't cost you anything to set up and will only take a small percentage from your sales.

The main advantage of having an online shop is people can view all your beautiful goods in one place. If they're interested in one piece, they might want to see a few more.

The second advantage is that usually the buying process is totally automated. You give the customer the information they need to make their buying decisions, and they hit the big 'buy now' button.

Marketplace sites like these include **Etsy, Folksy** (UK-only) or smaller specialist shops like **Weddings Made Beautiful**.

Facebook Shop section is slightly different in the UK (though not in North America), and there's currently no payment feature available, so if you want to have a go, you'll need another page or shop, like Etsy or wherever, so your customers can actually buy the goods.

If you would prefer to post and sell each item as and when you've made it, eBay is fun, easy to use, and you can really practice getting your product listings just right because you don't do them all at once.

All the sites, however, offer you the chance to provide information to your customers about your products. eBay has less information focused around the seller; Etsy and Folksy have more.

Let's look at these types of sites in a little more detail.

Etsy and Folksy-style 'shop' sites

Advantages

Transactions and shop functions are easy to use

All your goods are in one place, making it easy for you to add things, delete items, deal with refunds, sell your crafts, and communicate with buyers.

Shop promotion is a piece of cake

You can create product descriptions, a shop description or 'about' page, and add photos on-the-go, so promoting your products is way more convenient than you might have thought.

You can promote links to either the shop as a whole, or to individual listings.

Keywords are easy to use

Keywords aren't something to worry about; if you're being relevant, you'll use the right words in your product descriptions, and hopefully the site's search function will find them.

Disadvantages

Money

You'll have to pay a commission or transaction fee, and usually a listing fee (unless you choose to pay for a 'package' deal - we don't recommend this until you have a lot of items to sell, or you can guarantee you're going to sell a lot of gear).

> **For transactions**
>
> You'll need to be able to use an easy online payment system, and most sites prefer this to be PayPal or Stripe.

Lots of competition

There's loads of competition from other handmade artists and crafters on these sites, so getting noticed may feel a bit unsolvable. On the other hand, specialist sites might be the answer with smaller communities.

Time ... time ... time ...

Time is a major issue when it comes to setting up a shop. You have to upload pictures, write product descriptions, and set up your site, but you'll also need to catalogue your stock to keep track of everything. Don't forget to update your shop on a regular basis or it will become less and less noticeable to users.

Facebook Shop section

Advantage

It's what you know, and it's easy

If you're totally new to the game, and especially if you live in North America, Facebook Shop is a 'safe' option. Your business page will have trained you on how to follow Facebook instructions, so you'll find it pretty straightforward.

Disadvantage

Halfway there

Facebook Shop is a 'halfway there' option in the UK. It doesn't complete the sale then and there, so you risk losing the customer between leaving Facebook and going to your other shop to pay.

eBay and other similar 'auction' sites

Advantages

Easy-peasy system with very little pressure to produce

You can list one-off items whenever you feel like it, so there's no pressure to keep turning your stock around to make everything more exciting for potential customers.

Give yourself the option of a shop base or just sell one-at-a-time

You can build a shop if you sell more than 65 fixed-price items per month. It'll be comparatively less time consuming to sell lots through a shop than it will be to list them all separately as one-offs, but it isn't cheaper unless you regularly sell more than 65 items.

There's nothing to stop you diversifying into supplies and materials, mind. eBay doesn't care what you sell.

Start selling today!

You've probably used eBay already, so you'll be on reasonably familiar ground.

You can sell your goods just like anyone who's ever sold unwanted gifts or a piece of sports equipment ... and we're going to show you how to do it better.

Disadvantages

Stay away from auctions

We don't recommend using the 'auction' options. Given how much time, skill, love, and focus has gone into making your beautiful crafts, you don't want to risk selling them for just a few pence, so it's advisable to always select a fixed price for your products.

No shop unless you sell loads

eBay shops, and all the useful pages that go with those, are not worth doing unless you sell a lot of gear on a regular basis.

Prices for running a shop start at just over £20 per month, so you have to be sure you'll make that back (and a profit) before you start, or it will be more worthwhile to use the site for one-off sales.

A different kind of competition - how will you stand out?

You're not amongst a 'community' of other crafters and handmade artists; it's every man for himself. First, you're in a global market, so you'll contend with sellers from all over the world. But from a different viewpoint, you'll also compete with people selling cheap commercial gear as well as expensive handmade work. Try not to feel lost. eBay's given me my best successes yet.

How to sell better online

Regardless of how you proceed with selling your work, there are four basic parts to what you'll probably need to include (and only two if you just want to sell one-offs through eBay).

Help customers make buying decisions

You know what a buying decision is. It's the moment your customer thinks 'ooh, I'll have that', and clicks the 'buy now' button.

That click is the entire point of this book and of all your effort so far.

How you get your potential customers and visitors to the 'buy now' decision is down to how well you promote your products. The base of your promotion is the information you provide about your products. It's like a 'first tier' of promotion.

Shop name

Give yourself a catchy name if you like, but make it descriptive too. For example, my shop name on Etsy is 'CopperAndCoils'. 'Copper' describes the main material I use, and 'Coils' describes a strong aspect of my style.

Made-up or unusual words can work really well, but if they're hard to remember, it might be better to go with something a bit more straightforward.

> **Be memorable**
>
> It will be easier for your potential customers to search directly for you on Google if you use a shop name they can easily remember.

Tagline

Even professional writers find it a challenge to come up with the perfect tagline. Just go for it. Find words you like to describe your work, and try to create a very short sentence around them.

If you can give your customers a good idea of what your shop sells, in under 6 words (preferably 1-4 words), you're doing great. If it isn't catchy, that doesn't matter. It's more important that it's directly connected to your work. Most people prefer information to be easy to understand when it comes to a reason for them to spend their hard-earned money.

Try to make it as relevant to your work as possible. If you do lots of different crafts, use the word 'crafts' in there. If you do a very specialised type of craft, get that in there instead. E.g. Vintage-style sewing, or hand-thrown pottery.

Shop description and about

Most shops like Etsy and Folksy give you a page to say what you do, what style you use, your materials, and so on. eBay shops also give you room to do this.

You'll get differing amounts of space in which to write your description, so you may have to keep it short (Folksy with 400 characters only) or you may find you have more than enough room to write this (Etsy and eBay).

Product listings

When you post your products, either in your shop, or onto eBay, you'll want to give your buyers the information they need to make that buying decision. That's called a product description, and it's featured on your product listing.

Think about your product description in terms of 'what do my customers not know about my products?'

- **They don't know how you made it;**

and

- **They don't know how it will benefit their lives once they've bought it.**

Give them relevant information

Your customers don't want to know how many times you stabbed your finger with a needle or how many times you had to start the project over - they need relevant information about your product that helps them make the right decision for them.

'Relevant information' is a term used a lot in marketing, but what does it really mean?

Your customers want to know:

Is it well-made? What's your proof?

Your skill level, your attention to detail, your obsession with making indestructible children's toys, your CE tests ... All of this is relevant to how well-made it is.

Is it worth the money?

Consider your materials, the time it took you to put it together, the experience you've had as a designer and creator, and the problems it will solve for them.

This type of information will help your potential customers assess if they think your crafts are worth their hard-earned cash.

How will your crafts benefit your customers' lives?

Your pretty earrings or decorated glasses really will help make people's lives better! But to work out how, you'll have to get past how beautiful your creations are.

The people looking at your work already know they like it - they can see how gorgeous it is. But they've a lot of crafts and crafters to choose from, so how do you make a splash in their cash?

You stand out from others when your work means something to the people who look at it. Give it meaning by telling them how the important parts of your product will help them in their lives.

Breaking down products into features and benefits

We call the important parts of your product **features**, and the ways they help your customers' lives are known as benefits.

When you tell your audience how the important parts of your product will help them in their lives, you're using solid features that provide benefits to buyers. Instead of just giving your opinion about your product (it's lovely, it's funny, it's cute), you're giving solid information and real reasons for them to buy. This is so much more effective in selling than just telling people how excited you are about your products.

What are features?

To recap: features are the parts that make up your product.

We've highlighted all the different features in these sentences below:

- Handmade 4000-sequin waistcoat in purple and gold.
- Pretty floral handbag in waterproof fabric.
- Decorated glasses in green and blue.

Can you see what we've done here? When you write what your item is made of, what it does, or how it looks, you're stating its features.

Problem is, customers don't always realise why the features will help them. So you need to say why, too.

That 'why' is the all-important benefit.

What are benefits?

One good way to help figure how the features will help your customers is to ask yourself this one question:

What problem does my craft item solve?

If you can get your imaginative crafting head on for a moment, it'll help if you get inside the heads and lives of your customers.

Features

Benefits

The 4000-sequin waistcoat will make the customer stand out, so it'll be great for a bridegroom or a performer. Because it's handmade with love and attention, the sequins will stay on longer, so it'll last indefinitely if it's looked after.

The pretty floral handbag in waterproof fabric will be hard-wearing, so it will last longer than other bags. It'll save precious handbag junk from being ruined in the event of heavy rain or a visit to Glastonbury during a classic British summer.

The decorated glasses in blue and green could be cute mementoes of a happy day for all the guests to take away. They'll make someone's wedding truly colour-coordinated, or could provide the perfect gift afterwards for the bridesmaids (if they aren't all broken by then).

So, to recap, when writing your product descriptions:

- **Tell them how you made it**
- **Tell them how it will solve a problem for them.**

Biographies and profile information

Use every opportunity to tell the Internet what you do and who you are, especially on your own site or shop. Etsy Owner Profile and Folksy Profile Biography both let the buyer read about you to help decide if they want to buy your gear.

The more your craft is associated with your name, the better. Profiles add to the pile of information the Internet has on you, and that makes you easier to find if someone's looking for handmade socks, perfumed candles, or spray-painted flags.

So your biography needs to be only about your relationship with your craft. How long you've been together; how hard you've worked to make that relationship work and grow; how your love for knitting, bottle-making, or printing has improved your life.

Don't laugh. I couldn't live without mine. Use the notes space opposite, if it helps.

1. How long have you been a master of your craft?

2. How does it improve your life?

3. How does it improve the lives of others?

Tips for making fantastic product photos

At the top of your product descriptions, you'll be able to add photos of your craftwork. It's really important these are eye-catching and clear so Internet users notice them as they scroll.

Take pictures that stand out

I often use a red background (the lid of my laptop) for the first images of my new pieces of jewellery and that helps my images stand out, highlights the jewellery, and gives a feeling of brand. Many people find that they get a clearer image using a white background, however; it's your business, you can play with backgrounds and photos as much as you want!

Take close ups!

This is your customer's only chance to see the product they're buying. One of the biggest drawbacks for online shopping is not being able to touch and check products in person, so help your customers and show them every part of your work.

It's great practice to take a picture of the whole item, and then back it up with lots of detailed close ups, so your audience can clearly see the quality of the stitching, gluing, and twiddly bits.

Lose the zoom

Close-up shots are great, but avoid the zoom function on your smartphone. Zoomed-in shots are hard to keep still, and the quality will be terrible. If you want to take a close up, hold the phone camera right up to the item.

Use daylight where possible

Daylight is the best light possible for most items, and morning light is especially good for photography, so use that to your advantage! And it's free!

If you notice you have lots of very dark shadows on one side of your work, bounce the light back towards your product with a piece of white paper card.

You can also reduce the depth of shadows if you diffuse direct light by hanging a piece of thin white muslin or even lace blinds across the window or in front of the main light.

Take your time, and experiment with different colours and additional lights. It will all be worth it when you have great pictures to show off.

Avoid using substandard photos for any reason

Your images are the first thing most people will see when you promote your work on social media. That means you have to use the best images you have, otherwise your customers will just scroll on by.

So, checklist time!

Product photos checklist

- [ ] Perfect sharp focus?
- [ ] Easy to see what the item is?
- [ ] Clear image generally?
- [ ] Nice colours that work together?
- [ ] Good lighting with no black shadows?

If you can check off all the items on this list, you're doing great!

Signing your work - watermarks and signatures

You already know if you put a personal photo on social media, there's a risk someone might 'steal' it, and use it for their own purposes. But what if you could actually benefit from that 'theft'?

What are watermarks and signatures for?

Watermarks are those half-visible logos and names you see on copyrighted images to stop them being stolen and used elsewhere.

Signatures often have the same use. The idea is to place it so it can't be cut out of the image without losing a significant part of the picture.

You don't really have to worry about your ideas being nicked. It's better if more people see them. But the best part of this practice is they're great for ensuring your image can't be used without advertising your shop site or business!

Sharing is the mainstay of social media. It's part of the point. Shared products, whether they're fancy soaps or pretty things, are products likely to sell better. But sometimes the only way they can be traced back to you is if your name or the name of the company is visible.

So put your business name or web shop address on it. Or even just your name, and a nice big © if you want. Even your logo, if it has well-defined shapes and is easy to recognise.

Watermark tips

Watermarks shouldn't be so dark they obscure the image, but they can't be easily removed, even for Photoshop whizzes, so they're ideal for product pictures. The trick is to make it impossible for someone to cut your watermark out without damaging the most important part of the picture. It's perfectly acceptable to place a watermark over the image, in the centre of the photograph.

The whole point of a watermark is that it gets in the way.

You can place a watermark on an image in any number of different ways, depending on the software you already own. We like to use MS PowerPoint to do this as it is really easy.

Google "how do I put a watermark on a photo?" to find any number of useful step-by-step instructions.

It might seem like a lot of additional work to add a watermark to your photos, but you'll get quick at it, and it will be well worth it in the long term, because potential customers will be able to easily track you down, even if someone else posted the image.

Signature tips

If you're not keen on watermarks, no problem! You can easily add your shop name or your own name to your photo in a normal colour, using free and easy-to-use graphics apps like Paint.net and Pixlr.com. These are both pretty straightforward to use.

If the solid colour of the words hides some of your work, and you don't like that, the next best thing is to place your shop name so close to the edge of the piece of work that it would be impossible to cut it out without chopping off part of the craftwork in the picture.

How are you getting on?

There's so much work involved to get two social media accounts up-and-running, and an organised online shop, it's important not to feel overwhelmed.

If you feel as though this project is taking over your life, let yourself have a little time off. It's better to recharge your batteries and swing into new, creative action the next day, than to let it all get too much.

After spending this much time on anything, you'll want to see some results. In some ways, marketing is just like crafts. The next section is all about getting those potential customers clicking excitedly through your social media posts into your lovely product listings.

Henna-design products by Saddaf Hussain

Mendhi by Saddaf

fb.com/Mendhi_by_Saddaf

STEP 3

Get your audience to click through to your products

At its most basic, a strategy is just a plan. You decide what you want, how you'll get it, and then you do what it takes to get it done.

Do you like a coffee in the morning?

So boil the kettle, grab a mug, stir in your favourite coffee and enjoy it. Your strategy for getting a coffee worked out.

If you Google for information about marketing, you'll come across a huge amount of information all bound up in jargon. But often those complicated-sounding words have quite simple meanings.

'Strategy' is one of those words. Sounds fancy, but all it means is 'a plan'.

Now you're going to plan how you're going to get sales through social media.

You'll be amazed how much easier it is to keep your marketing going if you have even a simple plan to remind you what you're trying to achieve.

It doesn't have to be complex, just clear, so read on and find out how!

Prep Task 4: Make a marketing plan

Remember the notebook?

Open it up again, and find a new page, or just grab a pen and use the space provided on the next two pages.

1. What do you want to achieve with this marketing campaign?

Do you want to pick up some interest, get more likes and followers, or make some quick sales?

2. What can you give your customers to make it easier for them to engage with you?

Imagine the users - your potential customers. What do they need from you in order to chat with you, order from you, and be interested in you?

As well as priced pictures of your products, and images of your work, you can give them patterns and templates, new techniques, and interesting things to consider. This is all relevant information about what you do and what you love.

3. Plan your objectives

Give yourself two objectives, and build them up as you achieve them. Maybe you want to aim for 5 sales this month and 10 the month after. If you don't get 5, you can start again. If your sales are great from the get-go, aim to get as many as you can handle!

4. Now go!

Take your time, and keep all your ideas, even the rubbish ones, because you never know when you might find they come in useful. Something silly this year may end up being next year's big thing.

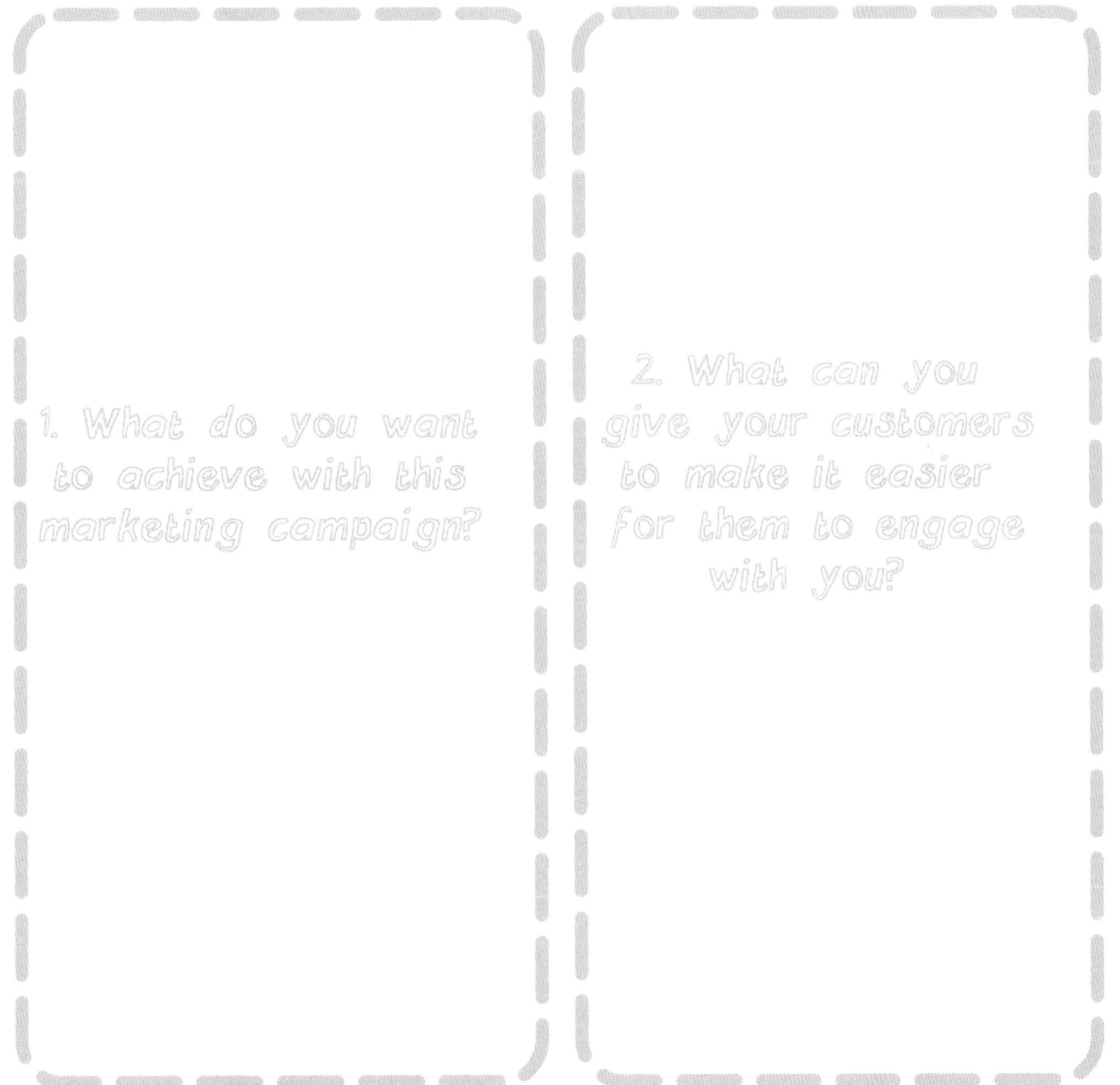
1. What do you want to achieve with this marketing campaign?
2. What can you give your customers to make it easier for them to engage with you?

3. Plan your objectives

Throw yourself into marketing

With your social media accounts squared off, you can concentrate on getting noticed by your ideal audience: potential customers.

You do that through a combination of three different methods:

- use eye-catching (but relevant!) images that shout "STOP!" as they scroll;
- give information that gets customers interested in what you're doing, and
- help them understand how your crafts might improve their lives.

It's easier said than done, but this isn't quantum physics. It's about knowing your audience and understanding - from their points of view - what makes them want to pay for something.

Social media marketing is a beautiful thing, done well. A post gets caught on someone's newsfeed, is spun across 10 more, and before you can say 'Zuckerberg', 60,000 people have seen it. But it's a long, long way from an exact science, no matter what all the guru marketers say.

You've got to be prepared to notice which posts get more likes, more clicks, and more comments.

When you spot one that does, you can use that as a template for new ones, and see if they work well too.

AIDA

It's not easy to predict how well a post will do, but marketers know some of the ideas behind why things are supposed to work.

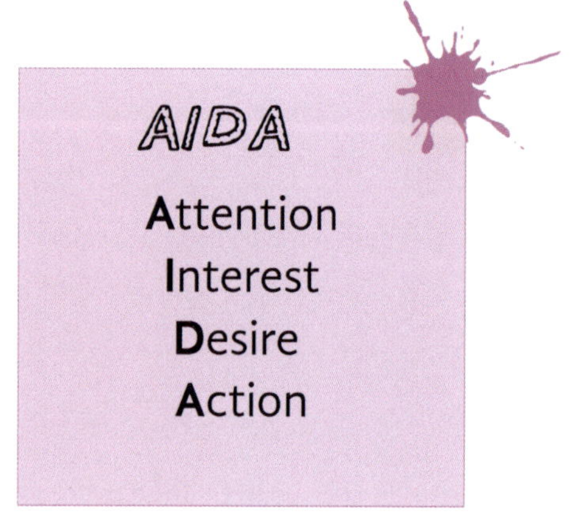

If you attract someone's **attention** and keep them **interested** for long enough, they'll end up **desiring** your product, enough to click the **'buy now'** button.

Marketers call this AIDA, to help remember it.

Get your goals straight

You don't need to sell-sell-sell all the time, but you must have a goal in mind whenever you post something new online. Having a goal makes your posts more effective.

You can say there are two very loose parts to selling through social media:

Engagement: your viewers comment, chat to you, message you, and share your posts.

Buying: your viewers want your posted item so badly, they've already got out their credit card or PayPal account to give you the money right away.

As much as 90% of your posts can be aimed to engage your users. You want them to react to your information, to comment on what they like, don't like, or have never seen before. You want them to tell their friends. Every time someone comments on a post, that action bumps the post up in their newsfeed - especially if they view their Facebook newsfeed through the 'top stories' order, rather than the 'recent news' one.

It also potentially bumps all the newsfeeds of the people who have liked it already, and in some of the newsfeeds of the people who liked your page.

That means every time someone comments, likes, or shares your post, there's a chance even more people will see it.

So most of your posts will have the aim to engage your viewers.

As few as 1 in 5 or even 1 in 10 of your posts should be an actual product that you are selling right now.

No-one really likes hard-sell; potential customers don't want to be shouted at, and they don't want to be sold to, or to be made to feel they should buy. They have a choice and expect sellers to remember that. Potential customers love information. By engaging them as one human being to another, you open up your own opportunities.

If you're nice to them; if they like you; if they understand the principles you work with - for example, if you're environmentally aware, or if you're really big on colour co-ordination or particular design principles or style - they'll be more open to buying things off you.

Successful posts are about harnessing your own humanness. They're about linking up with like-minded people who will appreciate your wares, and showing them more about why your craft is so cool.

So keep your goals in mind: do you want to engage them, or sell to them?

Pregnancy sells itself

Think about how a pregnant woman describes the feeling of her child kicking her. What her eyes look like. The expression on her face.

Those things combine to make all the women round her go broody, especially the ones who know how she feels. They all want one.

That's what you need to convey. The experience of your work and the love you have for it; put that across in your posts, because **that's** what they want to buy.

What should you post?

It's your crafting business: you can post what you like!

But of course, we've been telling you all along to remember:

- **What do customers not know about your craft?**
- **How will owning your craftwork improve your customers' lives?**

These same principles will dog you throughout the entire process, so you may as well get used to thinking in this way if you want to create effective social media posts.

That said, you can do this in any number of imaginative ways, and since you're a crafter, you'll have a head-start on imagination anyway. Goodness knows how someone in a drier, dull business would come up with this stuff!

We've listed below a few of the types of post that might work for you, and which, played together, will help keep your social media newsfeeds varied and interesting.

Progress pics and WIP updates

Your WIP is your Work In Progress. If it's going well, why not take a couple of pictures right now, and get that sweetheart on public view right away?

Sneak-peeks are intimate. They're like telling someone a little secret: "Look what I'm making." They stimulate interest, appetite, and may get the odd comment or two.

Progress pictures are especially cool for those of you who like to have several projects on the go at the same time. You know who you are!

This way, your page isn't waiting for an update for months - you can update it as you go - and some of your most interested viewers may keep checking back for updates.

It's a bit like serialising part of a book in a magazine, or even offering a sample view on Amazon. Piques their desire.

Unusual facts about materials or crafting process

When you haven't much to show, you can still talk about what you're doing, what materials you're using, and the techniques you like to use.

Share information. If you've discovered a new technique, share that webpage! Tell people where you found it, or if you discovered it offline, tell them which book, which workshop, or which instructor taught you it.

You don't have to feel afraid they'll go there and learn how to do it for themselves, because those people may not buy that particular item from you, but they'll learn to trust your information. They could pop back up one day. Everyone prefers to buy from people they trust. Long term, this sharing approach works wonders.

Some people may try to give that special technique a go, and when it doesn't work out for them, they may buy it off you after all. You never know what will bring your customers to your door, so go ahead and tell them a few 'secrets'. Your skill will shine through anyway, and competition's a fact of business.

Competitions and giveaways

Giving away gifts for free might rankle, especially if they've taken you a million years to make, but people love free stuff! You can totally use this to your advantage.

Create little things that take just a few minutes to complete, and do a giveaway on your page. A key ring, a pair of stud earrings, a pom-pom hat for a baby ... all these things have a value for people who use them, so handmade and free are bonuses! For the cost of postage, you could get yourself a few dedicated customers for life.

Create an interesting competition and offer up a nice prize as a sacrifice to the gods of marketing. You'll be amazed how many people check out your competition.

Competitions might help you get more people to like your page, but they'll generally be more successful if you have more people on there in the first place, so you may want to wait a couple of months before introducing one.

On the other hand, if you can make suitable items for competitions on a regular basis, why not have a monthly competition? This will boost your likes and shares every month, and has the potential to become really popular.

Blog posts

Blog posts are a special case for people who like to write a bit more. They provide extra value to your viewers, give them something to read and share, and help them get to know you better.

All of these things encourage them to think of you when they need a special gift for someone they love, or just to boost their own happiness occasionally.

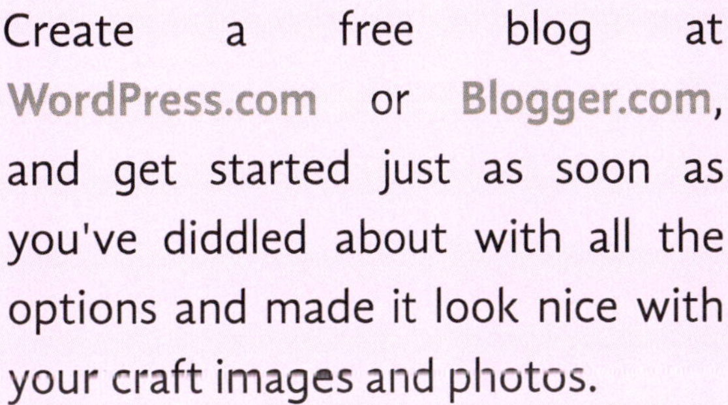

Blogging is free
Create a free blog at WordPress.com or Blogger.com, and get started just as soon as you've diddled about with all the options and made it look nice with your craft images and photos.

Write about what you do, how you do it, problems you've encountered, and why you love your latest piece of work.

Blogging isn't for everyone. If you find writing hard, or annoying, it won't be a fun job to do. Half the point of marketing through social media is to enjoy it, so don't blog if you don't love it. If you don't like writing, your blogs may sound forced, dull, flat, and uninteresting, and you could do your business damage rather than good.

There is another way, however, if you think it's worth having a blog (it is). There are millions of good writers out there on the web, and all you have to do is find them! You can get blog posts about your craft, written to order, from sites like Copify.com, PeoplePerHour.com, and Fiverr.com, amongst others.

All you have to do is tell the writer what subject to talk about, what style and tone you want, and give them any details you think should be included. On some sites, you can request a writer who is also a specialist in your craft.

These blog posts can be written reasonably cheaply, but remember you'll get what you pay for, so it's a good idea to aim to pay between £8-£20 per post. The more you pay, the more likely you are to get a good blog post written.

When it comes to thinking about goals, your blog posts are firmly sat in the 'engagement' seat. You want those posts to:

- Stimulate interested comments
- Be interesting enough to share
- Have a photo or image
- Be written clearly
- Have an interesting title
- Be no more than 2000 words, and definitely no less than 350.

In fact, people do prefer to read longer posts, so it's well worth writing (or paying for) 500-1000 words. Readers who stay the distance to the end are more likely to be potential customers.

New products and recently completed triumphs

And finally, you have the actual product posts. When you finish an item, and you're feeling great about it, take a picture, pop it online, and tell people how fabulous it is!

Give them a price if you're ready to sell it. Otherwise, just tell them it's coming soon on your shop, and they should look out for it. And don't forget to give them the link to your page.

Let people know why your product will improve their lives.

For example:

- Wow, I just finished these baby mobiles today! I can't wait to send the first one out, I just love to think of all those tiny babies out there watching my mobiles till they fall asleep!
- My first wraparound skirt of the season, and I've got all this wonderful fabric to make more! Cool days in a hot summer for all the pretty ladies!

Don't forget, you only need a tiny number of these each week or month, compared to all the engagement posts you put out there.

Don't sell, tell!

Tell them why your fancy photo frames will make a wonderful home for their wedding photos. Give them some images with your own kids, pets, or husband in your frames. Feed their imagination by showing what you would do with your product.

How to promote your Facebook business page

Facebook boosts and promotions are the biggest difference between the standard Facebook page, and the business page.

They turn every boosted post into a little advert for your page, and give you the power to increase your potential audience and gain likes from people who aren't remotely connected to you.

They're also relatively inexpensive, but you'll have to set them so the cost doesn't go over what you want to pay.

When you pay for Facebook boosts, you're paying for the reach every click and every 'impression' that takes place. An impression is when your ad scrolls up someone's newsfeed. As it crosses the screen, that's an impression.

When you pay for Facebook to promote your page, you are also paying for the reach. Reach is a little like a fishing net. Cast a bigger net, and you'll catch more fish. Reach describes the increased numbers of people who see your posts.

We're not going into the specifics here - it can get ridiculously complicated - and you're not spending enough money for it to really matter. It would be different if you planned to spend several thousand pounds on boosting your Facebook ads.

It's nice to have a few new posts on your Facebook page that are not promoted, before you begin the process of promoting the page and individual posts. That gives people who visit your page after clicking your ad something to look at when they land. They're basically the foundation posts on your page, and you'll get better at posting the more you do it.

Get a bigger reach

Reach is a little like a fishing net. Cast a bigger net, and you'll catch more fish.

Promote your page!

Get the best value out of your promotion

The most effective way to spend your money when you're only doing it on a small-time basis is to try to increase your reach. That means you're going to aim at increasing the number of people who see your posts.

People who like your page are more likely to see your posts - even if you don't boost the individual posts - so open your web browser, and type in:

fb.com/ads/create/

Click on **Promote your page.** 

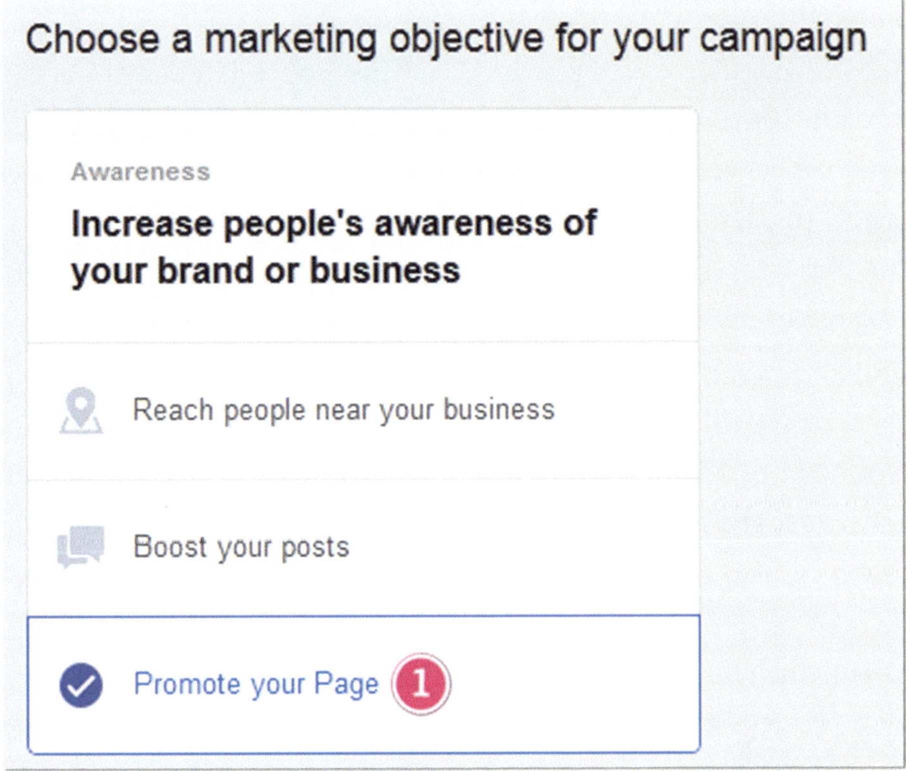

Select your page name

Click on your page name in the box that appears, and select the proper name of your page. It will show you your profile picture, which is how you know it's right.

Click **Continue**.

Define your audience

You'll recognise this next page: it's almost the same as the Preferred Audience screen used when you created your business page.

Choose the same options you already picked when you set up your page.

When you get to **detailed targeting**, type in the specific interests you want to aim for. For example, choose 'handmade soaps', 'handmade crafts', and 'online shopping'.

Where will your ad be placed?

You'll see a checklist that offers:

Mobile news feed

Desktop news feed

Desktop right column

Leave all these as the default - it's best to get your ad everywhere, rather than limiting it to only one kind of device or area.

How much, and when?

This is where you get to decide how much money you want to spend over how long a time. Play with numbers and dates until you're absolutely happy with the amounts.

Give yourself a daily budget. 2

Select **Set a start and end date** 3 or it will get very expensive indeed.

Select a sensible date to end your ad campaign. 4 We picked the very next day for the example, but as you become more confident about using the system and creating effective posts, you'll probably want to increase the number of days and run ads more regularly.

Make sure you're absolutely comfortable with the amount you're spending. You won't spend any more on this particular ad than what Facebook tells you at the

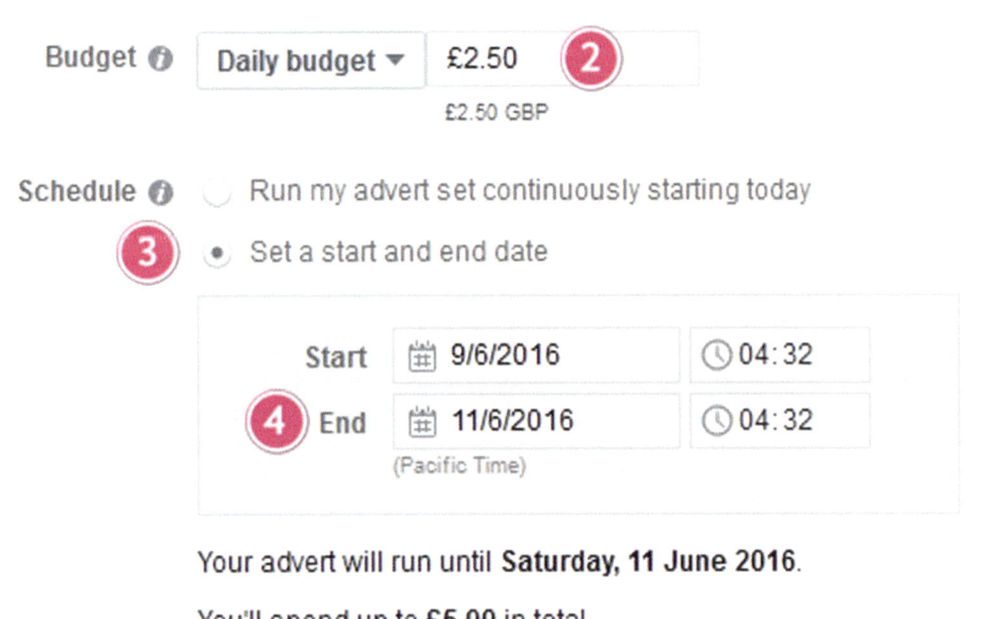

bottom. Here, you can see, it says we'll spend up to £5.00 in total, but the more you spend, the more people you'll reach, so only you can decide what amount is right for you.

Avoid heart failure

There's nothing like the heart failure you get when you think you've got a promoted post running indefinitely, so be sure you've set everything correctly, and then give it to someone else to check, if you're still not sure you've spotted everything you need to do here. You can guarantee when you have that horrible panic about it, you won't be anywhere near your computer or device to check it, so once again make sure you can afford everything before you finish.

Choose your ad's image

Select **Images**.

Choose an image that doesn't have any words on it if possible.

Click **Browse library** and upload an image from either your business page or your computer.

Select that image so it appears at the bottom under selected images.

Click **done**!

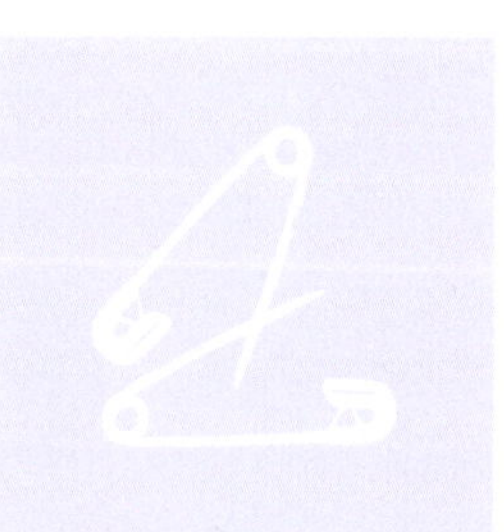

Write the right thing

This is where you get to really tempt your audience.

Type in the text 5 for your advert. You'll only be able to use about 10-15 words before they disappear into a 'read more' link, so make them count! Just keep changing it until you're sure you've got the right words in there.

Click **advanced options** and you'll see a headline box appear. Give yourself a useful headline that will catch your audience's attention. 6 Again, test out what it looks like on your ad - the headline will only show up on the Desktop Right Column image to the right.

Check what your advert looks like in all three locations by clicking on:

Desktop News Feed 7

Mobile News Feed; and

Desktop Right Column.

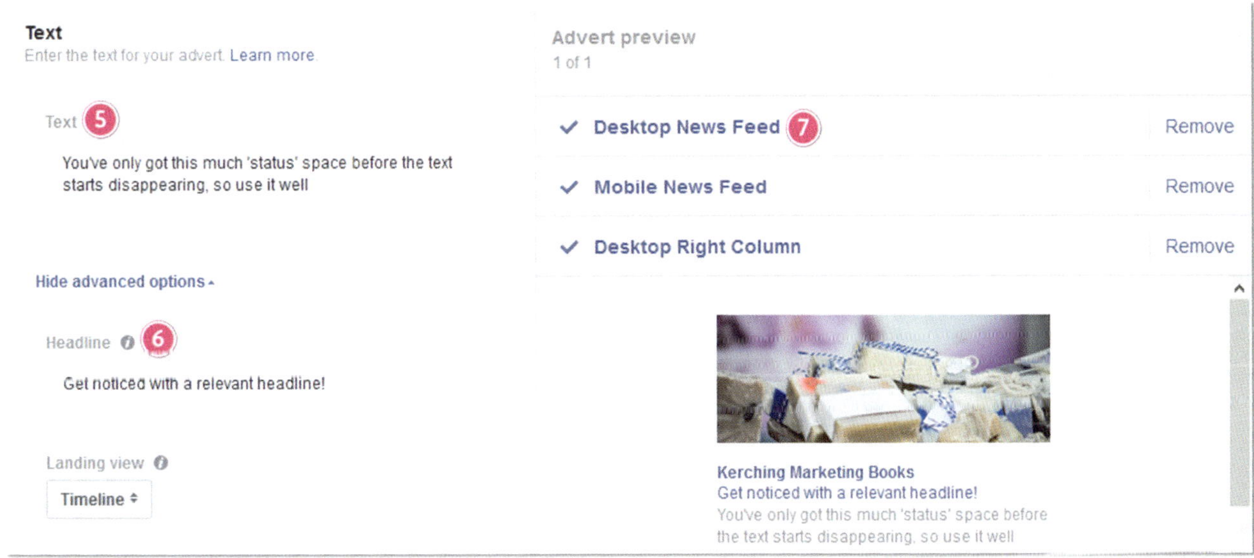

Carefully check your order.

Click **Review order** at the bottom right hand of the page (you may have to scroll down to see the button), and carefully check all your options again.

Happy?

Click **Place Order.**

That's it!

Images without words

Choose an image that doesn't use words, other than your watermark or signature. Facebook limits these on ads and it's therefore easier to use images with only pictures and no large-sized wordage.

Account Spending Limit

If this is your very first time creating an ad, you may be taken automatically to an **Account page** that asks you to set your **Account spending limit**.

Follow the instructions and set that to an amount you are sure you can afford when the time comes.

You won't have to pay this right away - Facebook bills you regularly, and you won't find you hit your spending limit very quickly anyway, and certainly not if you're only spending £5 here and there. £25-£50 is plenty for a spending limit at this stage in your craft business.

That spending limit is a failsafe to ensure you don't accidentally spend thousands of pounds if you forgot to set an end date in your promotion.

How to boost a Facebook post

Boost your business

Post boosts are the simplest way to promote your work on Facebook.

It works very similarly to Promote, but is a bit easier as you have fewer options to choose from.

Create the post you want to boost

Create a nice new post on your Facebook business page.

Click **Boost post.**

Set your audience

Click **Create new audience**.

Set your audience or leave it as defaults.

Type in all the interests you think your relevant audience will have. E.g. online shopping, handmade crafts, etc.

Click **Save.**

Set how long the boosted post should run

In the left-hand column, select the **duration** you want your post to run for as an ad. The choices are 1 day, 7 days, or 14 days.

Click **Set Budget.**

The screen will jump back to your business page with your post still showing as unpublished.

Get that post published!

Click **Publish Post.**

The post will be published after Facebook inspects it.

If you change your mind about something later, just click the **Boosted for £x.xx** button and alter the money settings. If you change the picture or the words, your post will have to go through the Facebook approval check again.

Facebook Analytics

Jump to your business page now, and click on the Insights tab at the top of the page.

You'll see a series of graphs and icons. Scroll down to the table that looks like this one:

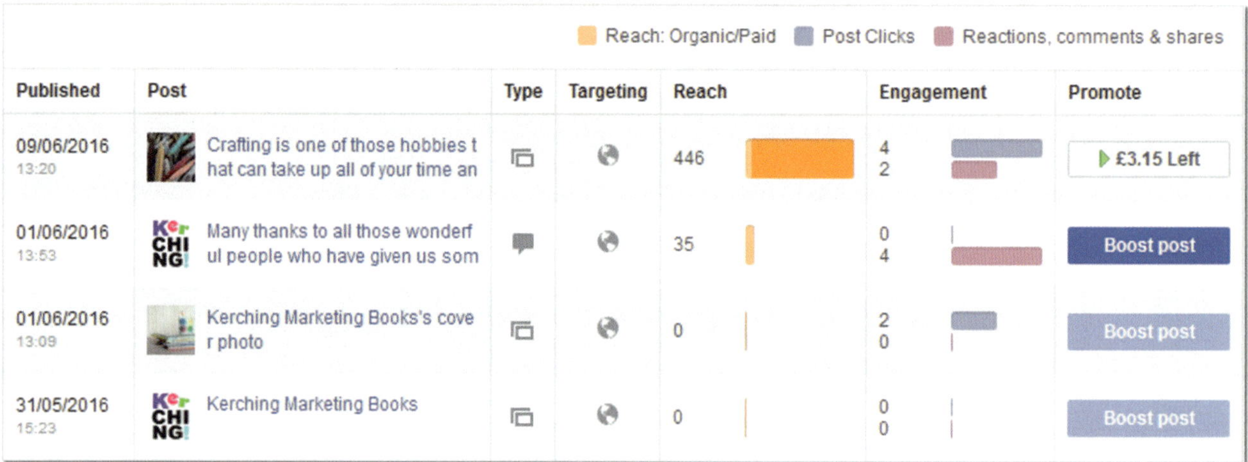

Reach: Organic/Paid · Post Clicks · Reactions, comments & shares

Published	Post	Type	Targeting	Reach	Engagement	Promote
09/06/2016 13:20	Crafting is one of those hobbies t hat can take up all of your time an			446	4 2	£3.15 Left
01/06/2016 13:53	Many thanks to all those wonderf ul people who have given us som			35	0 4	Boost post
01/06/2016 13:09	Kerching Marketing Books's cove r photo			0	2 0	Boost post
31/05/2016 15:23	Kerching Marketing Books			0	0 0	Boost post

Learn the terms

Remember, this isn't complicated information, you just have to know what the terms mean.

Reach

Reach is how many people scroll past your advert or post. Whenever your post or advert passes across someone's screen, Facebook calls that an 'impression'.

Organic

'Organic reach' is when your posts reach people without being promoted. That is, either you didn't promote the post at all, or you did boost it, but people who already liked your page saw it as part of their normal newsfeed, rather than it being a sponsored post. Light orange in the table represents those people.

Paid

'Paid posts' are those you have paid Facebook to boost, and 'paid reach' counts those people who saw your boosted post. It appears in their newsfeed as a sponsored post.

Post clicks

Anyone who clicks on your post is counted as a click. A click is an action - the user opened your photo and looked it properly, or visited your page

Reactions, comments, and shares

Facebook - after years of being begged to introduce a 'dislike' button - has given its users 'reactions'. You can still 'like' a post, but thanks to those nice Facebook designy-dudes, now you can also feel love, anger, wow, sad, and 'haha'.

This metric counts the numbers of reactions, comments, and shares that are made for each post.

Targeting

This is the audience you decided on when you set up your boosted posts.

Engagement

This column holds all your likes and shares information, including if they are paid or organic.

Analytics made simple

Like we said before, there's nothing complicated about social media marketing. It can get confusing at the analytics stage, but there's no need to get stressed out. Keep looking at the analytics table - especially at the posts you have paid to boost - and you'll find you understand it more and more.

Analytics Task: Analyse your own posts

When you think about why a post did better than others, ask:

How many words did I use?

- ☐ 16+ words?
- ☐ 11-16 words?
- ☐ 6-10 words?
- ☐ 2-5 words?
- ☐ 1 word?
- ☐ 0 words?

Which emotional words did I use?

e.g. happiness, regret, love, adore, terrifying, want, need.

Images

- ☐ Photo?
- ☐ No photo?

Type of post

Post was:

- ☐ A question
- ☐ A statement
- ☐ A link to a shop product
- ☐ A link to my shop
- ☐ A link to another site
- ☐ An offer
- ☐ Information about craft
- ☐ Work in progress

Record the information in your notebook, and from now on keep that pad just for this. If you're using a mobile device or tablet, that's great too, but make sure you can easily remember where you saved the document. The information in there will grow over time and you'll be glad of it one day.

When you notice a post does better than most, use the above categories to create a template.

For example, if all posts with a photo do better than those without, always include a photo or a graphic. Don't forget to keep them relevant.

Another example: if information about your craft gets you more clicks than product information, add crafting information to product shots, and provide a link at the bottom.

You can build a template this way, just from your own experiences.

Get ready to jump!

There's no escaping it now. You're taking the leap into marketing your own products and skills, and nothing else feels like it.

You're allowed to have the jitters in private, but when you're working the social media crowd, you'll reap more customers if you're cheerful, interesting, and positive.

If it makes you feel better, prepare a number of posts on a Word document, so you don't have to think on your feet at the time. All you have to do then is copy and paste them into the social media site you're using. For example, I started the marketing campaign for this book with 90 pre-written posts.

Usually you notice a glaring mistake the moment you launch, but don't worry, you can change things quickly and easily before anyone else sees it.

It's time to make some money.

Online marketplace for elegant crafted wedding products

Buy and sell to make every wedding beautiful

WeddingsMadeBeautiful.co.uk

Step 4
Sell your products!

Making sales doesn't have to be high-powered and aggressive.

You can just be yourself most of the time, and the customers you want will show up. Stay persistently available, rather than persistently selling.

If people really like you and the things you make, and you stay visible to them, they'll buy from you one day.

A big error many new sellers make is to believe they have to convince buyers that they want the products. It may seem logical, but it isn't quite right.

Buyers already know they're interested in the product. But they might have other possible options to choose from, such as products from your competition.

All you have to do is strike the difference from your competitors, telling your potential customers how your product - and only your product - will enhance their lives in a way they hadn't previously realised. Sounds complicated and difficult, I know, but stay with it. The more you do, the faster the penny will drop, and you'll be coming up with benefits automatically after a bit of practice!

You're preaching to the converted, so be friendly, be informative, be relevant, and give great customer service!

The nicest thing about content marketing

Content marketing is doing customer service better, and great customer service creates sales.

How to convert your visitors to customers

If you search Google for this phrase, you'll find a lot of marketing babble, where people who already do online marketing consulting try to teach other people who want to do online marketing more successfully.

But although their ideas probably work just fine for the marketing industry, the clever bits you need are much easier and cheaper to perform.

When you use social media for your marketing, you're content marketing.

Content doesn't have to be long, and it doesn't have to be only full-length blog posts. It can be good social media sites full of photos, comments, statuses, and the occasional video. The baseline of social media is sharing, so your content will also be useful or interesting links to other websites and content.

Content marketing works because it attracts attention, stimulates conversation and interest, and leads customers in by the hand. It takes a little while to get going, but it works if you persist. Keep writing posts; keep taking pictures. Don't stop! If your posts don't get attention, do them differently.

Content marketing is one of the most convenient forms of marketing, because you 'do' social media anyway. A line here, a comment there, and you're sorted! You don't have to set any special time aside; thank goodness!

See, although all those 21st-century virtual marketing methods work for people who want to spend their time marketing, if you'd rather be crafting, the old-style bricks-and-mortar shop service still works a treat.

The clothes shop analogy

If you work in a clothes shop and a potential customer comes in, you'll probably speak to her. Say good morning, how are you, that type of thing. You might ask her to let you know if she needs anything.

When the customer asks to try on a dress, you're encouraging. Positive, for sure. Maybe even suppressed enthusiasm. When she asks about the item, you're knowledgeable but not too pushy. You point her in the direction of some information about how the item is made and where it is from.

If she can afford it, she's probably going to buy it.

When it comes to turning visitors into customers, you're more likely to get a sale through good customer service, which includes genuine interest in your own craft and products, and giving relevant information.

'Relevant' means it's no good posting images of cute bunnies, the family pet, or anything too personal. If it's not something your customers might want to know about your work or your craft, it's best not to post it. Just like working in a shop.

When to sell what

Successful crafter-sellers seem to be particularly good at remembering dates and advertising their ideas ahead of time.

It's a great strategy and done in the right social media groups attracts leads immediately.

Remember holiday dates

If you want to be diligent about special dates like Mother's Day, Christmas, Valentine's Day and so on, mark them in your diary, mark the date of the last post you can send them so they arrive on time, then mark a reminder 3 weeks earlier. You let people know about your products suitable for that date, and make sure you stick to the last-post deadlines.

Birthdays happen all year round

Your work-in-progress and new-products-you're-proud-of pictures make lovely positive posts about your work, and keep you visible to interested viewers. You don't know what your potential customers' important birthdays are, but you know they have them, so it's just a case of keeping on with the posts, photos, links, and any other media you have.

A post or two a day about something/anything and a quick response to comments will be plenty.

Use Facebook groups

Facebook groups can have very narrow interests, which means if you get the right people at the right time, you may sell quite a lot of items when the time comes.

The trick is to offer a relevant idea to what has been asked for.

For example, if someone asks for a gift for a sight-impaired grandma, that sparkly frame with a loving quote in cursive probably won't sell this time.

If you stay relevant, you don't waste your own time.

Comment more

Making yourself visible on social media doesn't just mean posting all the time. Commenting is also good, and helps to bump other people's (and your own) posts up the newsfeeds. More people will see your input, the more you do it.

What's more, commenting means you get to test out opportunities. If someone wants to know information related to your craft, help them a little, or better still, direct them to a good website that answers their question. You've got nothing to lose and everything to gain from being friendly, interested, and knowledgeable.

Direct people as close to the goal as possible

If someone expresses an interest in your products, direct them to as near your 'buy now' button as possible. Your overall goal is for them to click 'buy now', or otherwise place an order. That means you want your interested customers as close to the goal as they can be. Heck, they want you to make it easy for them to buy from you.

But that doesn't mean plastering Facebook with links to your shop or business page; just if someone shows an interest in what you do.

If you have an Etsy shop, you can post your product pages, or if you take orders through your Facebook page, post that address instead.

The link implies they'll find out more if they click.

Better still, add your link to the end of a relevant comment, especially if you've been asked about price, product range, or crafting skills. You're giving them the chance to discover you.

The importance of genuine reviews

Yay for reviews!

Most people will get 5-star reviews on a regular basis, with the odd one that turns into a brief dispute, usually about returns or design.

Why your tiny crafting business needs reviews

Reviews are important, because what other people think can influence your buyers. Other people's opinions count, and they help potential customers work out if they want to buy something.

When it comes to buying products - especially handmade, specially-designed arts and crafts - the only way potential customers can check out what sort of experience they will have with you is to scroll through a few reviews.

How you respond to reviews is also crucial. If you get a negative review, particularly one you didn't see coming, it's advisable to get the conversation onto a private channel, like Messenger or email, as fast as possible. Stay polite, interested, and keen to make right, but remember some reviews are fake, and some claims for refunds may be fake.

Using reviews

Make the odd post with a gushing, happy, or funny 5-star review, and use the photo of the item you've sold to that person if you want to show off a little. There's nothing wrong with showing off your talent.

You can also use reviews for testimonials. Create a pinned post on your Facebook business page, and quote part of a 5-star review, or use it on your website if you get one made.

Don't forget to ask the reviewer if you can use what they said for your marketing.

The good, the bad, and the ugly review practices

It's fine to ask customers for a review after they buy something. Nothing wrong with it. It's not soliciting reviews, it's just sensible.

> **No soliciting!**
>
> Soliciting reviews is offering some kind of reward in return for a great review. It's not a good thing. Just give great customer service instead!

In fact, remind customers to leave a review, and you can even print cards with the review page address and include them in the packaging to jog their memories when they open their parcel.

You're not supposed to buy reviews in any way. Offering something in return for a good review is called soliciting reviews, and it can get you a bad reputation quickly. No prizes or anything else can offered in return for a good review. Only a great product, fast delivery, and lovely customer service will cut it.

And it's not considered good manners to leave fake negative reviews for other people, although the competition may seem strong in some crafting disciplines. Play nice, it will always work best.

It's better for your karma to work up a loyal band of happy customers with your own brand of good feeling.

Keeping the 'promise' you made on social media

Social media is located on the Internet, that special place where people can say what they want and no-one can stop them.

When you use it to market your work, you make at least 3 promises to the people you interact with:

1. **Your products will be beautiful and well-made;**
2. **Your delivery will be in time for their special event; and**
3. **The whole transaction will be smooth, easy, and fun.**

Sometimes things happen, and get in the way of these promises:

Other commitments: illness in the family; responsibilities; full-time jobs; job loss or change of circumstances.

Events beyond your control: bad weather; lost in post; missed the last post; ran out of yarn and had to start again; product damaged after it was sent.

Problem customers: whether it's a lack of communication; unrealistic expectations; or a frightening level of anger for some small issue, all customers are not created equal. And not everyone is reasonable.

Positive feedback

The more you stick to your promises, the more positively your brand and products will be viewed and reviewed.

The promises you make and keep become part of your brand. You may think 'I'm tiny, I don't have a brand', but really you do.

Do your best to stick to your promises, or problems will show up in your reviews, and that could lead to fewer sales.

Increase the chance of return trade

The best business is return trade: customers who come back over and over. That's what you want, so what do you do to achieve it?

It's simple. Be nice to your customers. It's the clothes shop scenario all over again. You're welcoming, encouraging, interested, and knowledgeable, so your customers will like you. Offer returns, 10% discounts, free postage, and anything else in your arsenal. Make every transaction happy for online shoppers and lots of them will return.

Service beats price

Customers over the age of 35 rate customer service as more important than price. Be reliable, and really, really nice.

Coping with criticism

Be nice, be understanding, and be ready to change things if something you do in the sales process doesn't work for your customers.

When it comes to your crafts, criticism can be great, especially when it's given in a nice way, but even if it isn't, there's no need to take anything personally. You can still be nice, even if someone is horrid to you. (I know how hard this is, right?!) Even if you can't believe they said that.

You have the upper ground. It's your product and you can choose to change it or keep it just the way you want. You can also block them in your social media profile settings.

For complaints about unexpected size of product, colours, or personalised details, you've got the sales process on your side. If you've tried your hardest; shown the customer exactly what to expect with good photos of your products; described sizes and colours and any other important detail in the product description; and honoured your sale agreement in every way, you can feel good about that, even if your customer isn't happy.

However, you still might be able to learn something useful from the experience. The result may be that you use signed-for mail for expensive items, pack the boxes differently, or add a 'fragile' label to the box.

Life-long learning is where it's at. No-one is too old to learn from experience. It's where common sense comes from.

The 'expensive' criticism - the only hack you need

One criticism you may often pick up is that your items are too expensive.

This tip came from an online marketer called Bushra Azhar, and it really works.

If someone says to you, "your work is too expensive." Ask them: "Compared to what?"

This is the greatest take-down ever for a really annoying and hurtful criticism. It forces the critic to explain their thinking, at which point you learn they know nothing about the crafting process, marketing, or how much materials cost, and they hadn't realised the almost identical items in Wilkos or Poundland were mass produced in a factory. It's awful and amazing what some people don't understand about producing handmade goods.

"Reasons" someone may give for your work being too expensive:

- It's made from bits of old tat.
- It looks like something made by a 5-year-old.
- I could throw that together in less than half an hour.
- I thought it would be bigger.

- I saw it at Wilko's for £2.99.
- Did you make it yourself? I can tell.

But whether they're pieces of copper jewellery, or wind chimes made from recycled materials from the countryside, no matter what you make, your products took you time, skill, talent, and effort to make. And there's a good chance they cost you money, too.

You decide how much your work is worth, not the people who visit your shop. If someone complains about your price, there is a strong chance they like your work but can't afford to buy it. It's okay to still be nice to them. No-one has to get hurt. You can let that fish back in the water. They were never your audience in the first place.

The Price Formula

LABOUR x TIME + COST ÷ QUANTITY + 20% PROFIT

= YOUR PRICE

A word about price

How much you charge for each item isn't a guess.

You can work it out, and if you repeat patterns and designs often, you only have to work out the cost once, not every time you make something.

You need to know:

- COST: How much the raw materials cost you.
- QUANTITY: How many finished pieces you made.
- TIME: How long it took you to complete all the pieces.
- LABOUR: Your hourly rate.

Multiply LABOUR by TIME.

Add on COST.

Divide by QUANTITY.

That's how much your product cost you to produce TOTAL COST.

You can then add on 20% profit, if you're feeling really brave: divide TOTAL COST by 100, multiply that by 20, and add it back onto TOTAL COST.

If you're uncomfortable with that price, it's cool to mess around with the hourly rate, and see how much you think your work deserves. The more accomplished you are, the better your hourly rate should be, but only you can decide what you should get from this.

Be fair to yourself

There's a fine line between being fair to your customers and selling yourself short. Be fair to yourself too, or it won't work.

Don't forget: you designed it, made it, and took the time to create something. Even if you're not completely expert yet, all those things are worth money.

Mailing problems

When someone tells you they never received your parcel ...

... You're not alone, whether you made a sale through Facebook, or your online shop. Even if you suspect the claim to be false in some way, you're usually covered as long as you follow all the rules in the terms and conditions carefully.

How they work will depend on the payment service you use, like PayPal, World Pay, Stripe, and so on, so read up on the terms and conditions, and especially look out for mentions of Seller Protection and Buyer Protection.

For example, if your buyer bought your product through PayPal's 'Goods and/or services' portal, in most cases they will be reimbursed, and so will you. It may sometimes be to PayPal's discretion.

Read all the terms and conditions you find, to start with. Once you know the gist of them, you can read them less often, but knowing your rights and position in the event of a dispute is invaluable.

Don't forget, legal stuff changes over time, so you will still need to read the occasional terms and conditions.

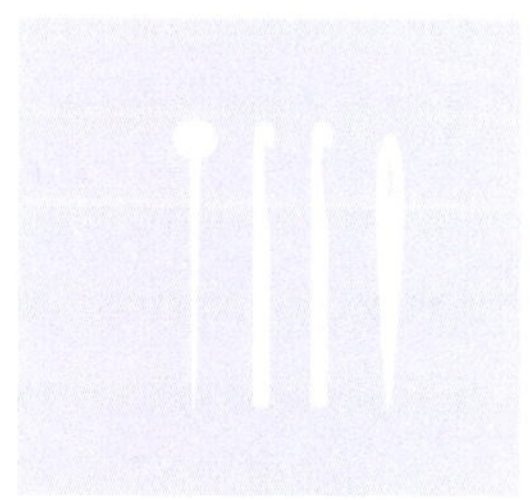

Good luck and congratulations

If you've made it through each step of this book, and you've got a Facebook page, a second social media account, and an online shop, well done!

This is a long hard (but fun!) slog, but it's absolutely worth it. It feels great to pay for things with money you earned from your own talents.

If you're worried your page isn't popular enough - don't. It's best to keep trying, stay cheerful, be persistent, and try to notice when you get something right.

The wrong things are often more memorable and easier to spot, but you deserve to realise when you've done well! Content marketing of any kind takes time, but it's seriously effective, and is what all the big guys do too. Why do you think there is so much information across the web these days?

Focus on engagement, and giving out lots of useful and interesting information, and your beautiful craft products will sell themselves.

Stay up to date in marketing

Nothing changes quicker than social media sites, so get yourself over to KerchingMarketingBooks.com/updates for free updates on the best social media sites for crafters.

Make the most of your microbusiness marketing with KerCHING's tips, know-how, and easy guides.

About Sakina

Sakina Murdock is passionate about three things: writing, crafts, and promoting other people's amazing talent. She doesn't believe in 'can't', only YES! NOW! and HOW CAN I DO THAT?

As the lead copywriter for a small international marketing agency, she's got the experience and know-how to show you how to market your handmade goodies with individualism and panache.

As a crafter with a microbusiness in handmade copper jewellery, she's been through all the TIME vs CRAFTS vs OTHER COMMITMENTS issues. And that's someone who already works in marketing. So that's what 4 STEPS TO SOCIAL MEDIA MARKETING FOR CRAFTERS is for: it's a guide to get you selling your goods without making too many mistakes or wasting too much time.

Sakina lives with her dog in the north of bonny Cumbria, and tries to stay out of trouble.

Ker
CHI
NG!

Printed in Great Britain
by Amazon